LOCKED-ON TEAMS

A Leader's Guide to
High Performing
Team Behavior

WILLIAM DUKE

Foreword by
James D. Murphy

Locked-On Teams

A Leader's Guide to High Performing Team Behavior

With Forward by James D. Murphy

William Duke

ISBN (Print Edition): 978-1-54397-956-5

ISBN (eBook Edition): 978-1-54397-957-2

© 2019. All rights reserved. No part of this publication may be reproduced, distributed, or transmitted in any form or by any means, including photocopying, recording, or other electronic or mechanical methods, without the prior written permission of the publisher, except in the case of brief quotations embodied in critical reviews and certain other noncommercial uses permitted by copyright law.

TABLE OF CONTENTS

Foreword	1
Introduction	4
L – LEADERSHIP	17
L1 – Take Responsibility	19
L2 – Get the right people on your team	24
L3 – Model Appropriate Behaviors	33
L4 – Cultivate Situational Awareness	38
L5 – Facilitate Collaboration	44
L6 – Delegate and Trust	50
L7 – Orchestrate Mutual Support	57
L8 – Thank and Reward	65
O – ORGANIZATION	71
O1 – Develop and Execute Standards	72
O2 – Align roles to goals	77
O3 – Measurements follow Intent	82
O4 – Establish a Course of Action	86
O5 – Plan for Contingencies	90
O6 – Establish an Execution Rhythm[SM]	94
C – COMMUNICATION	102
C1 – Establish / Reinforce organizational identity	103
C2 – Connect to the big picture	108

C3 – Brief Every Plan	112
C4 – Establish a Communication Plan	116
C5 – Listen Actively	123

K – KNOWLEDGE — 130

K1 – Take Action	131
K2 – Include expertise and diversity	135
K3 – Learn every day	141
K4 – Train and Develop	146

E – EXPERIENCE — 152

E1 – Red Team	154
E2 – Assess to Iterate, Improve and Accelerate Experience	158

D – DISCIPLINE — 164

D1 – Prioritize	165
D2 – Focus	170
D3 – Risk Smart	176

Conclusion — 181

Where to Point Your Finger First	181
What About Inspiration?	182
A Leadership Map?	183
Leading Forward	184

Appendix A – The Flawless Execution Methodology — 189

What is Flawless Execution?	189
Overview of the Flawless Execution Cycle	191
Overview of the Flawless Execution Model	193

Appendix B: Summary of Guidelines — 195

FOREWORD

Leadership. The word conjures up much emotion and visions of moving masses to great victories- overcoming enormous challenges and conquering a great goal. But, how does the word leadership help you? Especially now, in today's ever-connected, complex world of business?

Changes and pivots required in business today overwhelm old-school notions of leadership that direct people toward goals planned out in the C-suite. The industrial age of centralized planning and command-and-control hierarchies is in its twilight – almost, but not quite gone. Younger generations in the work force today expect more collegiality, collaboration, feedback and flexibility than the leadership styles of the previous century demanded.

It takes bold leaders to design, inspire, and align to create the future we all seek. Leaders that can see the future clearly and develop *pulling* rather than *pushing* mechanisms to get people, process, and technology aligned to move forward is the key to effective leadership in this new age.

If you are like most of my clients, you are struggling to identify good leadership practices and scale them throughout your whole organization. In the following pages you will realize that leadership is a lifelong, intentional journey, one that will require patience and effort. Whether you are young and taking up the mantle of leadership for the first time or a seasoned leader with many years of experience, fundamentals are always important to reflect upon and implement with sound judgment. You'll find those fundamentals within this book.

Leading a team through a challenge and then reaping the rewards of that collective effort can be one of the most satisfying and meaningful experiences of your life. I remember the first true leadership challenges and issues I undertook in my military and business careers, challenges that seem very similar to the ones I continue to take on today. Developing and holding myself to a standard; having the discipline to model that standard myself; and trusting others to execute those standards with integrity have been essential to my success, my team's success, and the success of the organizations I've led. Friendships are part of business, but as a leader the standard always wins - doing what's right and staying the course will test the best leaders. I know it has and will continue to test me.

In my military career I learned that *transformation* must occur in *you* and *your team* if you are going to lead and improve. I went from farm-boy to fighter pilot in sixteen months! Did the U.S. Air Force have to transform me and others? Yes – and it had to do it quickly in order to survive, thrive and dominate in our environment. That intentional process of transformation was, and still is, the key to success in military organizations around the world. Yes, leadership can be learned. The fundamentals of leadership are a set of interconnected patterns, processes, and techniques that can be scaled throughout an organization. However, there's no one-size-fits-all prescription that leaders may follow.

Leadership is a quest - a personal quest that you get excited about, that you dedicate real effort and mental focus to in every aspect of your daily life. Your own family will be a testing ground – so will your friendships. You'll find that many of the principles laid out in this book can be just as important in your personal and family life as they are in your work life. To truly become a leader, your skills must come from the deepest part of you day in and day out. Real leadership never takes a break or a vacation at work, home or at play! When you truly become a leader, everyone knows it. It's not a title you earn or throw on your shoulder. It's who you really are. Be proud of your leadership quest, it will shape you for the better, every day.

In the following pages William M. Duke will lay out the why, what, and how of leadership. The guidance within is built upon science, the experience of successful leaders, and the results of many years of practice and implementation. The principles and guidelines herein are not just based on our own personal leadership journeys, but upon those of thousands of client engagements that my team at Afterburner has worked through for over twenty years - leadership lessons and challenges the best CEO's, EVP's, Managers and Entrepreneurs have encountered. The lessons we have learned come from our clients in tech, retail, manufacturing, healthcare, and countless other sectors of business and even professional sports. This recipe for success is not just another leadership manifesto, it's real boots and leather experiences honed by elite military leaders applied and redeveloped in the halls of corporations and successful teams. You have in your hand the blueprints to your own effective leadership system. Strap-in! This leadership ride will *pull* you to the next level.

James D. Murphy

INTRODUCTION

There is no consensus among leadership scholars and practitioners on how best to define leadership. However, that should come as no surprise to those who have thought conscientiously about the subject. The effort to define leadership is meaningful. It's a philosophical struggle for those seeking to understand their place and responsibilities as leaders. For most, leadership does not become a subject of interest until one finds oneself in a leadership position. For such novices—and for experienced leaders alike—this book assembles the fundamentals of leading high-performing teams in a single, easily accessible resource.

The consensus on the definition of leadership rests on two characteristics—*influencing* and *goal-setting*. If a group of people already *want* to achieve a shared goal, that is best. If not, then leadership gets really tough. If the goals are counter to what the group wants or believes is right, then one may question if it is not coercion rather than leadership that is needed; power and control rather than influence and aspiration.

The fact that leadership resists simple definition despite the thousands upon thousands of books on the subject should not come as a surprise to those that have genuinely struggled to understand their role as a leader. That is because leadership, for good or ill, is about *affecting*. To *affect* others means to influence them emotionally. Many leaders throughout history have led without any formal power – such as Martin Luther King Jr. or Mahatma Gandhi. Often, they embodied a popular idea or desire and provided a focal point for the aspirations of many.

However, this book is not about leading or taming the colossal forces of transformative change at work today. This book isn't even about the transcendent and unchanging fundamental principles of leadership across the vast canvass of human history. Instead, this book is for those who find themselves, either by chance or by choice, functioning as a leader of a team in any organization. But what's more, it is for leaders today, here in the early 21st century, because circumstances change and societies evolve. Most leaders today—whether in a small start-up, a large corporation, a non-profit, a government agency, or even in the military—lead teams in a modern and mostly democratic knowledge economy. Historically, that is a different context than, say, leading a phalanx of Spartan warriors against an overwhelming Persian invasion at the Gates of Thermopylae almost 2500 years ago. It is also different from leading a Dutch East-India company trade expedition to Formosa in the 17 century. It is different from running a Ford Motor company factory in Detroit producing Model T's in 1920, and it will probably be different from leading any sort of organization in the early 22nd Century as well.

There is a joke worthy of note and reflection that characterizes the difference between leading teams today from just a few decades ago. "How do you know you are working in the twenty-first century?" The punchline: "Your boss doesn't know how to do your job." The point here is that managers hire specialized skill sets to do important work. These skill sets are often highly technical and perishable, requiring life-long learning (and re-learning) to maintain relevancy. That is the essence of a knowledge economy—to employ intelligent, highly skilled people to create and execute valuable products and services and establish their value in a global economy.

A subtle point one might notice in this joke is the use of the word "boss." It has become an antiquated term with a negative connotation. That is because two revolutionary changes have taken place. First, the shift to a knowledge economy is a shift in the value of the average worker from muscle power to mind power. We now value people for their mental and creative effort and their ability to solve highly complicated and complex problems rather than for their ability to do manual labor such as shoveling coal. Just as that shift has driven a much more egalitarian work culture and flattened hierarchies in most organizations, it has also created functional silos within large organizations that resist cross-functional cooperation and understanding. Alignment of effort across an enterprise can be challenging when specialized expertise erects functional boundaries.

Second, the objective of leadership has shifted. Previously, leaders were managers. Their objective was usually to get a precisely measurable productivity goal "out" of the people they employed, as though they were "squeezing" them. That is no longer the norm. Managers must be leaders. Leaders must align, influence, and care for their team such that the team works together as a whole to achieve an objective that no single member—not even the leader—is capable to achieve alone. The whole product or outcome a team seeks to create is greater than the sum of its individual contributors. Again, this is a revolutionary change, so much so that we don't use old terms like boss or manager to describe leaders of teams anymore. Instead, we use words like "coach" or "facilitator" if not the word "lead" or "leader" itself.

There is an acronym with a U.S. military origin that has become increasingly popular in modern business and is even taught in prominent business schools. The acronym is VUCA and it stands for Volatility, Uncertainty, Complexity, and Ambiguity. It's an apt acronym to describe our modern age. Change is volatile, disruptive, and rapid. The cascading effects of actions and activities within an organization and across the global economy are chaotic. Leaders struggle to identify what they and their teams should do and then must brace themselves for the unforeseen consequences of both success and failure.

But, there is a silver lining. We know more about how people think and behave than ever before. And since leadership is about *affecting* people, psychology is of central importance to the practice of leadership. That does not necessarily make leadership easier, it just means that the science of leadership is evolving. The application of science is technology – to put what we understand into practical application. Therefore, this book is a work of *leadership technology*. What the wheel is to transportation, this book is to leading teams in modern organizations. The aim of this book is to provide a fundamental component in the ever-developing *soft* technology of leadership.

Why *soft* technology? Leadership is often referred to as a soft skill. Soft technology is an attempt to provide substantial guidance to the exercise of leadership, a practice that is usually considered an art more than a science. We are living in an exciting time when the boundaries of our understanding of human behavior and cognition are expanding daily. Not surprisingly, most of that discovery is proving what conventional wisdom has directed for ages. But, that doesn't mean that leadership can be fully reduced to clear rules. At best, a set of structured guidelines emerge, each potentially inadequate across the full spectrum of contextual extremes. This book establishes and organizes those guidelines into an intuitive structure. It will define them, articulate the scope of their boundaries, and suggest specific actions for leaders to take to develop their teams into high-performers—to introduce greater firmness to the soft technology of leadership.

However, no leader can simply follow a set of prescribed activities and be fully successful. Leadership is a complex undertaking in a VUCA environment. There is no substitute for good judgment—knowing what to do and when to do it. There are circumstances that may demand an outright violation of the guidelines provided herein.

Only experienced leaders know when it is appropriate to develop and execute a different leadership approach.

Wax On, Wax Off

Think of this book as *Mr. Miyagi's Leadership Principles*. Who is Mr. Miyagi? The actor Pat Morita played the iconic Mr. Miyagi, a fictional character, in the 1984 film *The Karate Kid* co-starring Ralph Macchio. Macchio's character, Daniel, seeks out Miyagi—a martial arts master and World War II Medal of Honor winner—to teach him karate. But Daniel's initial experience is not what he expects. Mr. Miyagi tasks Daniel with a series of exhausting menial chores. In one scene, he instructs Daniel to wax his car in a specific circular motion alternating between his left and right arms instructing him "wax on, wax off." Additional chores follow suit such as scrubbing floors and painting fences with other highly prescriptive, repetitive motions. Daniel does not understand that Miyagi is teaching him the fundamental movements of martial arts. In an explosive scene, Daniel confronts Miyagi and accuses him of taking advantage of his eagerness to learn. At that point Miyagi poignantly demonstrates the value of what Daniel has learned by asking him to "show me wax car!" Daniel makes the wax on, wax off motions thus deflecting blows that Miyagi directs at Daniel. The lesson is clear, fundamentals come first. What Miyagi was teaching Daniel was muscle memory and the unconscious proficiency of movement necessary to master the style of karate Daniel wanted to learn.[1]

Fundamentals matter, but the mindless repetition of fundamental movements like Daniel waxing Miyagi's car are not enough in actual

---

1   Mr. Miyagi's pedagogical strategies would likely not work in the real world. Learning theory distinguishes between *near transfer* and *far transfer*. These terms merely express the capacity to apply relevant learning and skills to an unfamiliar situation. The motions of waxing a car as they apply to the martial arts is a *far transfer* situation which isn't likely to work. However, because the actions prescribed in this book are *near transfer* skills, they will.

martial arts combat. Mastery of fundamentals should ultimately enable one to employ and adapt such fundamentals in new contexts. The contents of this book are similar. The guidelines herein are fundamental, but without the judgment born of experience, mastery cannot develop.

In the real world, one of the most successful team leaders of all time, John Wooden—former head coach of the UCLA basketball team—won ten NCAA championships in a twelve-year period. He astonished players each new season by covering fundamentals as mundane as how players should put on their socks. In his time, his leadership style was considered unusual, but the results were unassailable. What's more, he was beloved by his players. His classic book on leadership is a must read for anyone interested in developing their leadership skills. But many of the actions and activities that Wooden undertook in daily practice and management of his team would not work in a modern corporate environment. Why? Because he led a basketball team in the 1960's. Although the fundamental principles he describes are relevant across a wide variety of enterprises, college basketball in the mid-twentieth century is different from leading the digital transformation of a global automobile manufacturer in the early 21st century. Context matters.

Culture is contextual and it matters, too. Michelle "Sonic" Ruehl, U.S. Air Force Academy graduate and pilot tasked with directing operations at night over Afghanistan, chose to volunteer and teach English to the local community by day. For Sonic, it wasn't just something to pass the time. Teaching English also provided an opportunity to build stronger relationships with the community she and her teammates were protecting by night. It was a strategic choice and it was a leadership choice. The challenge, however, was a cultural one. Sonic was a woman in a military uniform carrying a gun to class in a Muslim country. Upon entering the classroom, her students reacted fearfully. Teaching is a form of leadership. In most cases, the guidelines found in this book work in the classroom or the boardroom, but there isn't much specific guidance herein to address the challenge Sonic faced. Hers was a communication challenge – not just from a language barrier, but from a cultural chasm of understanding. What could she do to solve it? She brought her guitar into the classroom. She used music to bridge the gap, and it worked. The students relaxed and accepted her. Sonic's story exemplifies the challenge in mastering leadership beyond the fundamentals. But, communication, amongst others, is one of the fundamentals that readers *will* find in this book. How anyone uses the basics presented herein is part of the art and mastery of leadership.

Genesis

This book began in error. It began with the aim of creating a complete checklist of leadership activities that would generate high performance in any team. But, like an engineer attempting to create a perpetual motion machine, this author ultimately came to the realization that no checklist could address the challenges of leadership completely and accurately. Indeed, some of the principles and practices presented herein may be transcendent. They may be valid at any time or place. But, it's almost impossible to put one's proverbial finger on absolutes when one is studying leadership. Despite all the research and eons of accumulated wisdom, leadership remains difficult to define, codify, and prescribe. Nonetheless, this book makes the attempt, however imperfectly.

Decades ago, when I started on the path to become a U.S. Navy officer, a U.S. Marine handed to me a small, wallet-sized tri-fold card with a list of the USMC's leadership traits and principles printed on it. I kept that card and referred to it often throughout many years of military service. It is a great list and one useful to any leader. It is still in use throughout the Marine Corps today. However, it troubled me that the guidance it provided wasn't always easy to translate into daily action. The card provided broad and often ambiguous guidance. I wanted something more tactical. I wanted a checklist that I could refer to daily, checking off the items one-by-one confidently saying to myself, "Yep, I did that today." But I never found such a handy item.

After a short active-duty career aboard U.S. Navy ships, I transitioned to what would become a 19-year career as an officer in the U.S. Navy Reserve. During those two decades I served as a commanding officer (general manager) of two reserve units and in senior staff and operational positions across a wide variety of Navy mission areas. In parallel, I served in middle management and unit management positions in a Fortune 500 corporation for eight years, taught in a high school for two years, and took all that experience to a consulting firm for an additional twelve years. It's a broad range of leadership experience in many different contexts. But what astonished me regardless of context, whether in the military, in schools, or in business was the pervasive lack—whether from ignorance or incapacity—of managers to apply the fundamentals of leadership. On average, military leadership is superior to what I've seen in the private and public sectors. However, I have also seen terrible leadership in the military and extraordinary leadership in the business world. One thing is clear, although leadership may be inconsistent across the board—sometimes good, sometimes bad; it is mostly mediocre.

Over a decade ago when I joined Afterburner Inc.—a consulting firm committed to helping its clients accelerate individual, team, and organizational performance, I recognized a simple structure in use that expressed the attributes of high-performing teams. That's when I realized I had found the structure I needed to build the sort of actionable leadership checklist I had been looking for all my career.

As a high school teacher and in teaching and facilitating adult client teams, I learned that structure is critical to success. For many decades it has been referred to as *gestalt*, a German word for *structure*. Gestalt has been used as a name for theories in education, psychology, and even storytelling to describe a complex idea—that providing an organizational structure for a thing simplifies and organizes it for others to learn and employ while also creating something more valuable than the sum of its individual parts. This book provides a gestalt for practicing leadership in the spirit of a checklist.

Distilling down all the things a leader *could* do into a comprehensive and intuitive yet accessible list of things a leader *should* do—and make it short enough to list on one page—has been the goal of this book. It is the culmination of a full decade of research and refinement. Its final form is LOCKED-On Teams. LOCKED is an acronym that represents the structure of the guidelines. It stands for Leadership, Organization, Communication, Knowledge, Experience, and Discipline. Those six categories are subdivided into twenty-eight fundamental principles of high-performing teams. Further, those twenty-eight principles identify certain prescriptive actions that leaders and their teams may take to accelerate their performance.

The reader should notice that leadership is just one of the six principles rather than a rubric to encapsulate the whole list. The title of this book was deliberate. It is not *LOCKED-On Teams: A Leadership Checklist*. Instead, I chose to title it *LOCKED-On Teams: A Leader's Guide to High-Performing Team Behavior* because, as discussed within these pages, the leader may be responsible for the team, but they are not the only ones responsible for the team. Everyone on the team is part of success. The best leaders develop other leaders. Thus, this is a book about the behaviors of high-performing teams rather than just the behaviors and activities of their leaders. Great organizations develop leaders at all levels.

Flawless Execution[SM]

Not only was the genesis of this book in error—conceived as a checklist but evolving into a set of guidelines—it should have been written more than two decades ago. It should have preceded the more prescriptive and actionable details that have been codified in the Afterburner Inc. proprietary performance improvement methodology known as *Flawless Execution*. But that is not what happened. *LOCKED-On Teams* grew out of a need for a general set of categories to classify successes and errors in the debriefing process, a critical element of the *Flawless Execution* model. Debriefing enables teams to learn rapidly, iterate, and improve. But developing lessons learned from the *Flawless Execution* process model demanded a simple categorization system to both direct the development of lessons and to provide a common language for tagging and identifying recurring root causes. Therefore, *LOCKED* was developed in response to that need. Further, it provided the basic structure to move from the specific, prescriptive processes of *Flawless Execution* to the general, holistic guidelines that has ultimately evolved into this book. *LOCKED-On Teams* attempts to encapsulate all the activities of high-performing teams while *Flawless Execution* limits itself to the highly actionable, prescriptive, and repeatable processes that relate to goal setting, planning, execution, and learning. *Flawless Execution* addresses a lot. It is powerful, but it isn't everything that high-performing teams should do. So, instead of beginning with the general information of *LOCKED-On Teams* and proceeding to the more specific *Flawless Execution,* development has occurred in reverse.

If the reader has some prior understanding or training in *Flawless Execution*, they should not expect much redundancy of material in the main text of this book. Although there is some overlap, this book may stand alone. It may even be a first step toward exploring the *Flawless Execution* methodology in more detail. However, an overview for the curious is provided in *Appendix A*. Although the text refers to *Flawless Execution* within some of the guidelines that follow, this book leaves off where *Flawless Execution* picks up. It keeps to a higher level than the prescriptive processes of Flawless Execution, and at points even augments some of those processes with additional advice.

For more than two decades, Afterburner has been consulting and training to the *Flawless Execution* model, a performance improvement system that its client companies have often included in formal leadership development programs. That Flawless Execution has a lot to offer leaders is clear, but its greatest value is in acting as an *engine* to drive the complete and comprehensive *LOCKED-On Teams* structure. Flawless Execution provides many of the process-oriented activities necessary for high-performance. *LOCKED-On Teams*, however, expands beyond those activities to provide a holistic and comprehensive guide for high-performing teams.

Structure

This book is organized into six sections that address each of the six categories of the *LOCKED-On Teams* model. In order, the sections are leadership, organization, communication, knowledge, experience, and discipline. Each section is composed of an introduction and an explanation of the supporting guidelines. Often drawing upon the latest research and discoveries in the cognitive sciences, each concludes with actionable recommendations on how to apply the guideline daily. However, those recommendations are far from exhaustive. They are only a few applications like Mr. Miyagi's instruction to Daniel to "Wax on, wax off." Leaders should ultimately use their new-found knowledge and combine it with an ever-increasing foundation of experience to develop their own applications in their unique context.

Below, the categories, fundamental principles, and actionable recommendations are summarized in the order they appear. Thus, this book can be read cover-to-cover, but also be used as a daily reference for improving team performance. In the spirit of a checklist, the reader may use the structure below to quickly find the guidance needed to coach a team daily. On a further note to the reader, the behavior of high-performing teams is complex. Many activities inter-relate and build upon one another. Thus, throughout the text frequent references may be found in one guideline to other guidelines. Therefore, a simple system of coding has been introduced for ease of reference. Each guideline is assigned a two-character code: a letter followed by a number. The letters correspond to the primary category of the guideline while the number simply references its order of presentation within that category. For example, K4 corresponds to the fourth principle in the knowledge category "Train and Develop." These codes are included in parentheses throughout the text.

What follows is a list of the twenty-eight guidelines in the order they are presented. Appendix B provides an expanded list that includes summary actions prescribed for each guideline.

LEADERSHIP

L1 - Take responsibility

L2 - Get the right people on your team

L3 - Model appropriate behaviors

L4 - Cultivate situational awareness

L5 - Facilitate collaboration

L6 - Delegate and trust

L7 - Orchestrate mutual support

L8 - Thank and reward

ORGANIZATION

O1 - Develop and execute standards

O2 - Align roles to goals

O3 - Measurements follow intent

O4 - Establish a course of action

O5 - Plan for contingencies

O6 - Establish interactive *execution rhythm*[SM]

COMMUNICATION

C1 - Establish / reinforce organizational Identity

C2 - Connect to the big picture

C3 - Brief every plan

C4 - Establish a communication plan

C5 - Listen actively

KNOWLEDGE

K1 - Take action

K2 - Include expertise and diversity

K3 - Learn every day

K4 - Train and develop

EXPERIENCE

E1 - Red team

E2 - Assess to iterate, improve and accelerate experience

DISCIPLINE

D1 - Prioritize

D2 - Focus

D3 - Risk smart

L – LEADERSHIP

"Leadership is an art that is made comprehensible by process."

- Christopher Kolenda, Leadership: The Warrior's Art

This book circumvents the age-old argument about whether leadership can be taught. Its assumption is that leadership is both art and science—that leadership and management are two sides of the same coin. On one side are the complicated knowledge and 'hard' skills of managing and on the other, the complex 'soft' skills of leading. At heart, this book is about the intersection of leadership and management, a place where processes and rules of thumb can be articulated and taught to generate and sustain high-performing teams. Leading requires an understanding of human emotions and motivations. To be a good leader, you must be emotionally intelligent. You must master the 'soft' skills which many managers find to be the hardest thing to do. Emotional intelligence is not easy to teach. Developing your emotional intelligence—or EQ—requires experience and the practice of compassion.[2] Furthermore, quality leadership is

---

[2] Author's note: the word 'compassion' is used rather than the commonly used 'empathy'. These words are not synonyms. The difference between them is critically important in effectively understanding others and responding to their needs. This difference will be addressed in C5 – listen actively.

also distinguished by its ethical dimension. Human history is filled with tales of great leaders who engaged multitudes to pursue wicked ends. Those leaders were effective at engaging emotions, but they led others to catastrophe.

There is a single quote that stands above all others about the ethics of leadership that serves as a guide. It comes from Rear Admiral Grace M. Hopper, USN (1906—1992), a computer science pioneer. She made the ethical responsibility of leadership clear when she said that, "You manage things; you lead people." Things are objects to be used. People, however, are subjects to be respected. They are things-in-themselves with their own purpose. They should not be used as objects or things.

This division between things and people is a fundamental historical shift that happened in the 20th Century. Western-style democracies began to respect individuals as subjects rather than objects. Before this shift we used words like management and labor to distinguish between knowledge workers and hired help. This is the 21st Century. Everyone contributes their knowledge and experience to getting the job done. We are all knowledge workers. Leaders must treat everyone with respect and value them for the contribution they make. Leaders must make sure that everyone is engaged in shared success.

This first section of the *LOCKED-On Teams* guide concerns the most "soft" and complex skills leaders should master with respect to the ethics of leadership. People, whoever they are and whatever role they play in an organization, expect fair and just treatment. They expect their voice to be heard. They also expect their leaders to guide them toward a better future or a compelling goal, or both. Leaders who can act ethically and cultivate ethical behavior throughout their organization create a tremendous advantage for themselves and others. It doesn't guarantee success, but it certainly removes barriers.

There are aspects of leadership that are unquestionably artistic. These aspects defy simple description or explanation. However, there are techniques and behaviors that experience—and in some circumstances even science—tells us are quite straightforward and therefore teachable. Leaders can execute some actions and activities that directly improve our team's performance. This "L" section of the guidelines is the largest section of the book because of the complexity of the notion of leadership. But the eight guidelines and subsequent actions detailed for each will help advance anyone further down the road to mastering the art of leadership.

L1 – Take Responsibility

> *"Our response-ability is a direct expression of our consciousness and free will. To be an effective leader, in fact to become fully human, you need to become fully response-able."*
>
> *– Fred Kofman*

Take Responsibility is the first item in the *LOCKED-On Teams* guide. It is also the most important. Without it, the rest of this guide is useless to you. You must own it. You must commit to *being* a leader rather than just occupying a title. If you cannot make that commitment, then put this book down. Give it to someone who can commit. For the sake of those you have been positioned to lead, it is this author's hope that you will also lay down the responsibility of leadership and defer to someone else with the necessary commitment to being a good leader.

If you can commit to taking responsibility, you are ready to begin becoming a better leader. These two words—*take responsibility*—are chosen carefully. You must *take* it. It can't be *given* to you. Leadership is an act of will. But to be a great leader you must do more than just take responsibility. You must expand the scope of responsibility from the limit of your personal self to the actions and performance of your team. That's an idea best described by former U.S. Navy SEALs and authors Jocko Willink and Leif Babin. They call it *extreme ownership* and describe it as the bedrock principle of great leadership in their book of the same name.[3]

Can you be a leader and fail to take responsibility? Of course! History is filled with stories of irresponsible leadership. Not all leadership is good leadership. Leadership is value neutral. At the expense of making a trite comparison, Adolph Hitler *led* others into a cataclysm. The reverse could be said of George Washington. It begs the question – what is leadership? Is responsibility an inseparable quality of leadership? I argue that it is not. If someone holds a gun to your head and commands you to do something you don't want to do, especially something immoral, unethical or contrary to your personal values or the espoused values of the organization you serve, that is not leadership. That's coercion. This is an important distinction for any student of leadership: leaders *influence* others to act. Coercion or control is *not* leadership. It takes followers for there to be a leader. If you influence no one, then you are not a leader however hard you may try. But, if you do influence others to act or think in emulation of your example, then you *are* leading – for good or ill.

If you accept that influence without force is an essential quality of leadership, then you must also realize that power, whether through force or social position, is not. Anyone may be handed the position and power to control or coerce others (and that should be a bit unsettling).

---

3   Willink, Jocko and Leif Babin. *Extreme Ownership: How U.S. Navy SEALs Lead and Win.* (St. Martin's Press, 2015).

Good leaders understand that taking responsibility for how they lead and what they both consciously and unconsciously do to influence others is what defines their character. Good leaders are mindful of what they say and do and act responsibly for the consequences of those actions.

Here is a simple experiment that demonstrates how leadership is in its crudest form a capacity to influence others. In the next business meeting (preferably one where participants are seated around a table) take a moment to stare at the ceiling. What did others do? How many people in the meeting, seeing what you did, looked up at the ceiling? We are social animals. We respond to behavioral cues. We unconsciously mimic each other. As you have probably known since you were a child, yawns are contagious.

As this book goes to print, Derek Sivers' TED Talk titled "*How to Start a Movement*" has over 7 million views. In it, he uses a video of a "dancer" to demonstrate how "a lone nut" (as Sivers describes him) can influence a crowd to join him in what is little more than an alcohol-induced flip and flail. Within minutes a huge crowd gathers around the dancer and imitates his performance. Is this an example of leadership? In terms of influence it is important to recognize that we as a species are highly sensitive to what Charles Mackay illustrated over a century and a half ago in his classic work "*Extraordinary Popular Delusions and the Madness of Crowds*". We humans are highly susceptible to developing a herd mentality. One of the central tenets of this book is that leaders bear a responsibility to leading rationally and with responsibility. Perhaps glancing at the ceiling or dancing wildly in a public place isn't burdened with ethical considerations. But, there is no clear delineation between imitation as innocent fun and a harmful, viral movement.

Good leaders bear a responsibility for speaking and acting appropriately. Anyone can lead by influence. Only good leaders wield the power of influence with responsibility and with purpose. Good leaders do not hide their motives. Good leaders are not manipulative. They do not use falsehoods or rely solely upon misguided emotions to influence a group to action.[4] Instead, they define a purposeful vision, represent it clearly, use reason to articulate its value, and recruit others to join them. They endeavor to lead honestly and with eyes wide open to the consequences of the effort they lead. They are mindful of the immediate and long-term results of both success and failure.

Furthermore, good leaders take responsibility for the actions of their followers. That is the idea behind a captain's responsibility for everything that takes place aboard his or her ship. As a former Captain of a U.S. Navy nuclear-powered aircraft carrier with a crew of nearly five thousand sailors once shared, "There are a thousand things that could go wrong every day that would get me fired that I have no direct control over." Similarly, Napoleon Bonaparte has been credited with the proposition that "There are no bad soldiers, only bad officers." Good leaders understand that their influence *is* their power. They don't rely on the power of their position to lead. Using positional or hierarchical power is coercive rather than influential leadership.

In his research and through vast experience, best-selling author and one of today's most respected business consultants, Ram Charan, discovered that good leaders *wanted* to be leaders.[5] They didn't just get promoted into leadership roles because they believed it was the path to success. Fred Kofman—Advisor of Leadership Development at Google and author of *The Meaning Revolution*—punctuates the same notion. "If you want to be a transcendent leader," he writes, "you need to accept full accountability for your actions in any circumstance, even

---

4   Dalio, Ray. *Principles*. (Simon & Schuster, 2017). pg. 464. "One thing that leaders should not do, in my opinion, is be manipulative. Sometimes leaders will use emotions to motivate people to do things that they should not do after reflecting clearly."
5   Charan, Barton, and Carey. *Talent Wins*. (Harvard Business Review Press, 2018). Pg. 62.

in circumstances that are not of your doing."⁶ Good leaders choose the responsibility for leadership. It's a willful journey. They do not just fall into it for the money or prestige.

This bound tome of ink and paper (or electrons) can only persuade the reader to become a responsible leader. It cannot compel or coerce responsibility for the actions of leaders or the madness of crowds. But, it is the first and best place to start everyday in the quest to become a genuinely good leader. Humans may be irrational and often join the herd in its pointless and unfortunate wanderings, but they can spot a faker quickly. Going through the motions and imitating the habits and actions of good leaders isn't enough. Good leaders are genuine leaders. That does not mean you always share how you feel or pretend to care about what you really don't. Sometimes good leaders do have to play along with the herd so long as it's not contrary to the vision they represent. We will revisit these topics throughout the course of this book. But good leaders cannot pretend to be something they are not. Hitler, after all, believed he was right and many shared his belief. It was the same for Washington. A good leader may be evil, a poor leader good. Leadership is a double-edged sword. Careful you do not cut yourself or others.

ACTIONS:

Reflect. Start your day reflecting on your personal responsibility as a leader. Unlike the items that follow in this guide, taking responsibility is an attitude that drives all other actions. The level of responsibility that you take can be felt or sensed either implicitly or explicitly by others. Taking responsibility is not an action, it is a commitment.

---

6 Koffman, Fred. *The Meaning Revolution*. (Currency, 2018). Pg. 8.

Lead Upward. Take the advice of Willink and Babin's concept of *extreme ownership*. Do not blame the boss when they don't respond the way you want or expect. Instead, blame yourself and then act to address it. "Examine what you can do to better convey the critical information" they assert. "To do this, a leader must push situational awareness (*L4*) up the chain of command."[7] Organizations are ultimately decision-making machines that turn decisions into actions. It's everyone's responsibility to share information and build knowledge so that the best decisions and actions can be made.

L2 – Get the right people on your team

> *"In fact, leaders of companies that go from good to great start not with "where" but with "who." They start by getting the right people on the bus, the wrong people off the bus, and the right people in the right seats. And they stick with that discipline—first the people, then the direction—no matter how dire the circumstances."*
>
> – Jim Collins, Good to Great

> *"The Army is not made up of people; the Army is people . . . Living, breathing, serving human beings."*
>
> – General Creighton W. Abrams

An organization *is* its people. Beyond the people, an organization is nothing more than empty cubicles, blank laptop screens, vacant point of sale kiosks, idle forklifts, and office-park ghost towns. The people are the point. Organizations serve and are composed of people. People are

---

[7] Willink, Jocko and Leif Babin. *Extreme Ownership: How U.S. Navy SEALs Lead and Win.* (St. Martin's Press, 2015). Pg. 237.

the source of value creation for an organization. They *are* the strategic advantage of a firm.[8] Who is on your team or in your organization matters more than anything else.

Putting together a team starts with the leader. Who will lead the team? Will it be you? Or, will it be someone else that you select to lead a team to accomplish some pre-determined goal? If the former, then you should very definitely *want* to lead the team. If the latter, then you should pick someone that is clearly committed to leading the team to success. The best leaders *choose* to be leaders.[9] They have both the self-confidence and the desire to lead, and a commitment to the purpose the team has been assembled to realize.

Commitment implies that the leader values the purpose of the organization. The leader must view the goal to be achieved as aligned with—or at least not in conflict with—their personal system of values. The same goes for the members of the team. Values must not conflict—not between the team and the purpose, or even between team members. Ray Dalio—founder of Bridgewater Associates, one of the most respected and successful hedge fund management firms—sees values as an essential, aligning force in an organization. "People who have shared values and principles get along," observes Dalio. "People who don't will suffer through constant misunderstandings and conflicts."[10] You can't just randomly throw people together unless you expect random results. The results of randomized teams are likely to be mediocre, less often outstanding, and from time to time disastrous, perhaps even violent, especially when values come into conflict.

Beyond aligned values, what else matters in selecting the right people? Of course, knowledge and experience come to mind. That is

---

8   Charan, Barton, and Carey. *Talent Wins: The New Playbook for Putting People First*. (Harvard Business Review Press, 2018). Pg. 3.
9   Charan, Barton, and Carey. *Talent Wins: The New Playbook for Putting People First*. (Harvard Business Review Press, 2018). Pg. 62.
10 Dalio, Ray. *Principles*. (Simon and Schuster, 2017).

what resumés and *LinkedIn* profiles exist to express, right? Those are also important and will be addressed later in the *K* and *E* series of this guide. But, before those qualities, consider diversity.

Everyone is different from everyone else in physical, experiential, and cognitive ways. It seems obvious, but there is a premium to be gained through selecting people to join your team with an appropriate level of diversity. However, it is important to first understand what kind of diversity matters and under what circumstances. Diversity is a hot topic, but it is currently on everyone's mind from the standpoint of inclusiveness rather than for its problem-solving value. Inclusiveness is important for organizations because of its social justice and demographic representation value. It matters because it is usually best for the people that make up an organization to physically look and behave according to a set of values that reflect the constituency or client base it serves. Beyond that, diversity's value lies in variation in the cognitive realm. So, although everyone is different, how they *think differently* is what really matters.

Humans are not cogs in a machine as they may have been in centuries before. We do not hire people into organizations solely for their capacity to perform work in a strictly physical sense. We get machines to do that. We bring humans into our organizations to solve problems and make decisions that machines cannot. Fundamentally, we hire people for their cognitive abilities. This is because the problems that need to be solved in the modern economy are complex and rapidly changing. Furthermore, these problems usually cannot be solved by a single talented individual. They require teams to solve them.

For complex or highly complicated challenges, cognitive diversity matters. "Diversity trumps ability" is the mantra of University of Michigan Professor of Economics and Complexity, Scott Page.[11] That

---

11   Page, Scott, *The Difference: How the Power of Diversity Creates Better Groups, Firms, Schools, and Societies*. (Princeton, 2007). Pg. xiv.

seems counterintuitive, but as Page has argued, it is a mathematical fact. To illustrate the idea simply, let's say you hire Jim to work in a factory doing nothing but pulling a lever and picking up a molded piece of metal to toss into a bin—over and over again, day after day. For a large factory, you might need hundreds or thousands of Jims. If all the Jims you need are exactly the same, production becomes a highly manageable and predictable process. Yay for the process managers! But the jobs we need humans to do are no longer like this. If you are launching a new product or service for the first time, you need a team with a wide variety of talents and experiences. Even if you have seven Einsteins, just one will be enough because the unique problem-solving power of a single Einstein is not increased with the addition of more Einstein clones. Duplicating a mind simply gives you the same thoughts and ideas multiple times. Nothing is gained. Diversity matters where new or different ideas are needed to solve problems. Thus, the greater the number of differing perspectives you have on a team, the greater the likelihood of that team generating a viable solution. Who would you choose to solve a crossword puzzle: the smartest person around, or the next five smartest people? Think about that for a moment and you will understand why diversity trumps ability.

Page discovered that ". . . diverse groups of problem solvers—groups of people with diverse tools—consistently outperformed groups of the best and the brightest."[12] Not always, but most of the time, diverse groups came up with better, more innovative solutions than like-minded groups. So, instead of forming a team of five newly minted Harvard MBA's, form a team of one Harvard MBA, perhaps another from Stanford, a third from Wharton, a fourth from MIT's Sloan School, and then maybe a fifth from a less prestigious program in the Midwest. Cognitive diversity matters because each member brings a different set of problem-solving skills and experiences from

---

12   Ibid. Pg. xxvi.

MBA programs that approach education in a different way—all other factors remaining equal, of course.

This guideline overlaps with another guideline: *K2 - Include expertise and diversity*, which the reader will discover much later in this book. Why divide the two? This guideline deals with team formation and is concerned mostly with alignment and values. That is what is important for the long-term success of the team. Guideline *K2*, however, addresses solutions and innovation and the often *ad hoc* nature of problem-solving on a daily, weekly, or monthly basis. *K2* helps leaders solve today's challenges whereas, this guideline is about building the future with a balanced and committed team.

Now, with a leader, alignment around values, and a list of diverse attributes as a recipe for success, you are ready to find as many people that fit these criteria as possible for your team, because more heads are better than one, right? Wrong. Believe it or not, you can have too many people on a team. As a general rule, keep teams small. You only need as many people on your team as you need to get the job done. Keep in mind that the optimal team size, confirmed through empirical evidence and witnessed everywhere in human organizations, is between five and nine members. Smaller than five, and complex challenges are difficult to master due to lack of cognitive diversity. Greater than nine, and teams become difficult to lead due to the complexity of the communications and relationships that must to be managed between members. Amazon has made the 'two pizza rule' part of its culture of small team formation. The implication is that no team should be larger than can be fed by two large pizzas.[13]

There are certain thresholds at which human relationships become unstable. Much like heavy atoms on the bottom of the periodic table decay into lighter ones because they are too massive to hold

---

13   Dyer, William G., W. Gibb Dyer, Jr., and Jeffrey H. Dyer. *Team Building: Proven Strategies for Improving Team Performance, 4th Edition.* (Jossey-Bass, 2007). Pg. 33.

together, large human groups fall apart as they grow. The five-to-nine-member composition of a team is intuitive because it occurs naturally and can be observed in most all human organization. But company or firm size is much more ambiguous.

How big can a company be? For some time, experts settled on what became known as the *Dunbar Number* named for anthropologist Robin Dunbar. The Dunbar number limited stable human groups to just 150 persons. But Dunbar extrapolated the data from his work with primates rather than humans. The actual limit is believed to be much higher. Most military units in which its members can maintain stable personal relationships is in the 450 to 500-person range. This corresponds to the size of the crew of most navy ships, infantry battalions, and aviation squadrons. Correspondingly, the U.S. Bureau of Labor statistics defines a small company as one with less than 500 employees. There is clearly a natural drive toward organizational communities that reaches an optimal limit at around 500 persons. More recent research has established another limit at the 1,500-person range. This number appears to be the limit in which any one member of the organization can recognize a face or a name. Hewlett-Packard famously divided its company when it reached the 1,500-person limit and this appears to be supported anthropologically as the maximum size of prehistoric villages.[14]

The lesson of size simply underscores that teams can only be so large because the need to communicate and cooperate quickly becomes unmanageable at a certain point. High-performing teams must exercise two-way communication between individuals. The formula $n(n-1)/2$ where n is the number of people on the team expresses how two-way communication quickly becomes burdensome and ultimately impractical. For example, a team of five requires ten channels of two-way communication while a team of nine requires thirty-six. A team

---

14   Karlgaard, Rich and Michael Malone. *Team Genius: The New Science of High-Performing Organizations.* (Harper Business, 2015).

of twenty members, however, requires 190! As team size grows, the communication burden grows much faster. Human cognitive limitations and the time required to communicate one-to-one quickly limit the capacity of teams to coordinate and communicate as they grow. So, don't just add people to a team. Keep teams lean.

Once you have identified an optimally-sized and diverse team, you have to "build" it. Team-building is a well-known phrase that is often viewed as a soft, nice-to-do activity rather than a critical step in team formation. Humans are social beings. They need to build trust and familiarity before the individuals can synergistically come together to complement each other's abilities and form a 'whole-greater-than-the-sum-of-its-parts' team.[15] Team-building requires some focused activity—usually fun, but still related to the mission or objective of the team—that provides an opportunity for team members to socialize.

As best-selling business guru Jim Collins has said metaphorically, you have to "get the right people on the bus" before you engage them as a team to accomplish a mission, project, or task. You cannot get where you want to go without the right people.

ACTIONS:

Pick a leader. Remember that the best leaders choose to be leaders. Promoting someone to be a sales manager because they were good at sales is a poor determinant of success. Selling and leading a team are different skill sets. It happens all the time— people get promoted mostly because there is a vacancy to fill and managers feel that promotion into higher positions is the right way to reward someone. It is called the *Peter Principle*. "In a hierarchy," write Laurence J. Peter and

---

15   Dyer, William G., W. Gibb Dyer, Jr., and Jeffrey H. Dyer. *Team Building: Proven Strategies for Improving Team Performance*, 4th Edition. (Jossey-Bass, 2007). Pg. 8.; Edmondson, Amy. *Teaming: How Organizations Learn, Innovate, and Compete in the Knowledge Economy* (Jossey-Bass, 2012). Pg. 12.

Raymond Hull, "every employee tends to rise to his level of incompetence." The best leaders don't let that happen. Instead, they develop others to take a leadership position when appropriate and merited (*K4*).

Align attitude and values. Recruit for alignment of values and an interest in the task, project or mission to be accomplished before you recruit for skills! Know what your organization's mission, vision, and goals are and seek recruits that view them as important. The more people you have on your team that care about purpose and goals, that have realistic rather than idealistic expectations of success, and above all, those that demonstrate strength of character will push out those that lack such qualities.[16] Allow the whole team—not just the leader or hiring manager—to evaluate candidates in the hiring or selection process.

Seek diversity. Team members should complement each other's skills and experiences. Everyone should contribute something different. Here are some important points to keep in mind:

- Networking is a great way to recruit. However, be careful to ensure you are identifying appropriately diverse candidates. Humans tend to gravitate towards other humans with similar backgrounds and interests. Recruiting friends onto a team may *reduce* diversity.

- When you don't have an opportunity to form a new team or replace weaker members, there are some proven methods to boost team performance. The *Kohler Effect* states that weaker team members working alone increase their performance when working together with higher-performing individuals. So, good leaders can orchestrate ways to match stronger and weaker members to raise the performance of the weaker. New research has shown that simply adding a single high-performing (hi-po)

---

16   Dalio, Ray. *Principles*. (Simon and Schuster, 2017). Pg. 341 & 414.

individual to a team can raise the performance of the whole team by 5-15%.[17]

Stay lean. A million employees does not a team make! Recruit only enough people to get the job done remembering that an optimal team size is five to nine people for a sufficiently complex challenge. Additional people with no clear roles or tasks to perform are likely to drag performance. There are natural limitations on the size of an organization before re-organization and restructuring may be needed to maintain optimal performance. They are approximately:

- Team – 5-9 people
- Small company or unit – 450-500 people
- Large organization or division of a larger organization – 1,500 people

Build the team. When a new team is formed, and periodically over the life of that team, take time for teambuilding. The best teambuilding occurs away from the workplace so team members can relax and detach from their work responsibilities.[18] Teambuilding should be fun and nurture one-on-one positive relationships. A teambuilding session should start with introductions between each member at least sharing names and job titles. But sharing personal information can really boost camaraderie.[19] One technique is for each member of the team to build a timeline of their life and spend five to ten minutes each telling their biography—the high points and low points of their lives. However, the best teambuilding should teach team members something valuable and/or contribute to the mission or values of the organization. So, take the team out to assemble bicycles for the local children's charity your

---

17 Chamorro-Premuzic, Adler and Kaiser. "What Science Says About Identifying High-Potential Employees." *Harvard Business Review*. Oct 2017).
18 Dyer, William G., W. Gibb Dyer, Jr., and Jeffrey H. Dyer. *Team Building: Proven Strategies for Improving Team Performance, 4th Edition*. (Jossey-Bass, 2007). Pg. 81.
19 Zak, Paul. *Trust Factor: The Science of Creating High-Performance Companies*. (Amacom, 2017). Pg. 52.

organization supports. Engage in a teambuilding activity that teaches basic planning skills. Sign the team up as a group for a communication skills class. Teambuilding should be a social, trust-building, and learning activity to be enjoyed that isn't specifically 'work.' However, simply having fun with the team in a social environment isn't teambuilding. By themselves, trust-falls and ropes courses are poor team building experiences unless coupled with mission-oriented learning or quantifiable outputs.

L3 – Model Appropriate Behaviors

> *"My life is my message."*
>
> – *Mohandas K. "Mahatma" Gandhi*

Modeling appropriate behaviors means several different things. It means that you demonstrate through speech and action how you and others should best serve the organization and its mission. How well leaders behave is critical to establishing a strong organizational culture. Just as professional actors pretend to be someone else to play a role, leaders must often act and speak in ways that are different or even contrary to their personality and opinions. Leaders must act according to the needs of their role.

Much has been spoken and written about the need to be an authentic leader. Playing a leadership role may be contrary to being authentic, a popular notion in leadership literature. Leading is about serving a purpose outside yourself that, from time to time, may contradict your preferences, but not your values. You cannot lead in an organization that pursues a mission or requires behaviors and actions that are contrary to your personal values. As in guideline *L1- Take responsibility*, if your values conflict with the organization, step down.

If you cannot act a leader in the context of the organization, its culture, and its values, then lay down the mantle of leadership and get out. Conversely, if there is someone on your team whose values conflict with the organization's, get them out. It is exhausting and burdensome to try and change someone's deeply-held set of values. You must consider the cost in time and effort that will likely be spent in vain.

If you believe in the mission of the organization, then you can act as a leader within it. As a former military commander who played a leadership role in various units, this author sometimes disagreed with policies and more often with the cultural artifacts and traditions that had accumulated for more than two centuries. Behind closed doors I often challenged policy and tradition, but never in front of my unit. My role was to support the big picture, purpose, and mission, to communicate that often to my team, and model the character expected in my circumstances—to smile and be gracious when I was otherwise chaffing under those expectations. No organization is perfect. Progress is always possible, however slow. A good leader is a prudent leader that doesn't naively tilt with windmills when their energy is better spent on supporting the mission. A good leader knows when to challenge and when to not, but also to always represent the values and the mission.

Peter Senge, MIT Sloan School of Business professor and author of the classic *The Fifth Discipline* said it succinctly: "The core leadership strategy is simple: be a model."[20] His student and author of *The Meaning Revolution*, Fred Kofman, followed up with a similar thought. "The transcendent leader is like a flag. People don't fight for the flag itself, but for what it symbolizes."[21] "In sum," asserts the Center for Creative Leadership's Handbook, "people endorse a leader who is the epitome of the group, so it is often harder for an individual who is not

---

20 Senge, Peter. The Fifth Discipline: The Art and Practice of the Learning Organization. (Currency, 2006). Pg. 162.
21 Kofman, Fred. The Meaning Revolution. (Currency, 2018) pg. 247.

considered representative of the group to be seen or to see himself or herself as a leader."[22]

History is filled with successful, yet inauthentic leaders. The mercurial Elizabeth I of England stands out as a prime example. She courted nobles but never consented to marry, thus maintaining an independent reign. She pretended to be heartbroken over the execution her cousin, Mary Queen of Scots, an execution she ordered to preserve her own life and the peace in her kingdom. And yet, she played her role well enough to ward off invasions and other catastrophes while maintaining religious freedom and prosperity for the realm. History and literature have praised her successes for centuries.

Jeffrey Pfeffer, in his excellent book on leadership which he tongue-in-cheek titled *Leadership BS*, claims that "In fact, being authentic is pretty much the opposite of what leaders must do. Leaders do not need to be true to themselves. Rather, leaders need to be true to what the situation and what those around them want and need from them. And often what others want and need is the reassurance that things will work out and the confidence that they are on the right track."[23]

In a poignant passage from David Garrow's Pulitzer prize-winning biography of Dr. Martin Luther King, Jr., King tells of a moment where the burden of leadership became overwhelming and he called upon God to give him the strength to persevere. "... And I prayed out loud that night. I said, 'Lord, I'm down here trying to do what's right. I think I'm right. I think the cause that we represent is right. But Lord, I must confess that I'm weak now. I'm faltering. I'm losing my courage. And I can't let the people see me like this because if they see me weak and losing my courage, they will begin to get weak.'" This quotation

---

[22] Velsor, McCauley, and Ruderman. The Center for Creative Leadership Handbook of Leadership Development, 3rd Edition. (Jossey-Bass, 2010). Pg. 150.
[23] Pfeffer, Jeffrey. *Leadership BS: Fixing Workplaces and Careers One Truth at a Time*. (Harper Business, 2015) pg. 87.

comes from a sermon delivered by Dr. King. Did he actually make that prayer using exactly those words or is he portraying a role and moving his audience to steel their courage in the face of violence? Was it just rhetoric? Does it matter? It's clear that King did indeed demonstrate courage in the face of dangers and indignities, not only to himself but to his family. That is a matter of fact. So, King both spoke and acted as a leader in the role he played. Leaders must accept that the mission or purpose they serve is larger than them. It is their duty to act the part that the mission requires. Leadership is a lot easier, however, when personal interests and values are shared with those of the organization.

Every adult should recognize that we humans are constantly looking for models to emulate. Employees watch their boss's behavior as a cue to how they should or might behave. And, of course, they are looking for signs of what they can get away with. They are looking for hypocrisy—a difference between what is said should be done and what is actually done. That gives them license to behave in an undisciplined manner. For clarity and accountability's sake it is best for behaviors to be codified into standards. Both discipline and standards will be treated later in this book.

The key word in this guideline is *appropriate*. What are the appropriate behaviors of a leader in your organization? Remember the 'dancing nut' from *L1 - Take responsibility*? His behavior is simple—dance like no one is watching. In the video, you can observe him showing the first person that chooses to join him how to do it. From there it catches on and a huge crowd joins in. What is appropriate for you as a leader in your organization is going to be a lot more complicated. Your first action may be to define those things if you do not already know what they are. In *The Best Place to Work*, Ron Friedman writes, "Every human organization is an ecosystem. All it takes is a single spreader to start a virus."[24] Leaders must be that spreader. The culture

---

24   Friedman, Ron. *The Best Place to Work: The Art and Science of Creating an Extraordinary Workplace*. (Perigee, 2014). Pg. 216.

the organization needs to be successful is principally shaped by the organization's leaders.

ACTIONS:

Put on your uniform. Put on your 'uniform' every morning before work. Assuming the mantle of leadership should be an intentional act everyday so that you are better able to stay in your role as a leader and act the part. The military uniform and the symbols affixed to it is a powerful reminder for any leader in military service. Soldiers, sailors, airmen, and marines behave differently in uniform than out. They walk taller, treat people with greater respect, and more willingly bear the burden their profession demands. What can you put on each morning that will function as an ever-present reminder of the role you should play? Is it a hat, a ring, a jacket, or just your access badge? Perhaps a memento you can carry in your pocket to touch frequently throughout the day to help you remember your commitment to modeling appropriate behaviors?

Call out behaviors. Call out others for demonstrating appropriate behaviors and call out yourself for *not* demonstrating appropriate behaviors (refer to *E2 - Assess to iterate, improve and accelerate experience*). But, never perform the reverse. You should quietly demonstrate the right behavior but be transparent when you fail to do so yourself. At the end of the day, stop and think about what you did wrong and what someone else did right to model appropriate behaviors. Share that with your team. If it was someone else that modeled an appropriate behavior refer to guideline: *L8 - Thank and reward*.

Commit publicly. Make a commitment to an act or goal. Do it publicly before your team and execute it. Just as Cortez burned his ships upon landing in the new world so that his troops would be motivated to conquer the Aztec empire, making public pronouncements backs you into a corner. You will have to model the appropriate behaviors to succeed or submit to your failure, learn from it, and move on.

L4 – Cultivate Situational Awareness

> *"All things can be deadly to us, even the things made to serve us; as in nature walls can kill us, and stairs can kill us, if we do not walk circumspectly."*
>
> – Blaise Pascal

Mushroom management is a problem in modern organizations. What's mushroom management? Humorously, the Urban Dictionary defines it as "to keep your employees in the dark, and every now and then throw shit on them."[25] This author encountered the mushroom metaphor many decades ago in military service—a little dark humor to lighten a common frustration. One might think that communication lies at the root of such frustration. But, the failure of information to be passed to the right people isn't always just about information transfer. Sometimes information defies simple verbal explanation. In some situations, information extends into the non-verbal realm where the other senses come into play. The people within an organization need to understand as best they can not only what is happening, but what has happened and what is likely to happen. They need a multi-dimensional sense of their environment so they can make the best decisions possible to direct their actions to create the effects that they and their leadership desire. They need an acute *situational awareness or 'SA'*.

Keen SA is essential in modern organizations because tasks are completed by groups more so now than in the past. And it is unusual for SA to develop naturally. So, it is the leader's responsibility to ensure

---

25   Farks_me. www.urbandictionary.com. September 18, 2003.

that everyone they lead has accurate, relevant, and timely information, and that the information is shared appropriately, not just from leader to the led, but also between team members and from the team upward to its leadership. Leaders need timely and accurate information—as well as opinions and judgments—from members of the organization that are at the front-line of operations so that they can make better strategic decisions. Situational awareness is a holistic quality expressed up, down, and across the hierarchy of the organization.

The failure of leaders and their teams to develop good situational awareness is *not* simply a failure to communicate. Poor situational awareness often arises from the failure to recognize the *need* to communicate. Poor SA is the result of self-absorption—the failure to recognize that you, the individual, are *not* the team—that the team is bigger than you and that it is not self-aware. That is not to say that some high-performing teams such as Navy SEAL teams have demonstrated levels of hyper-awareness that coordinate with near perfection and an almost supernatural SA. Such teams are certainly rare exceptions.

Most teams experience poor SA. The U.S. Coast Guard conducted a meta-analysis of boating accidents and found that poor situational awareness was the most commonly recurring root cause. Specifically, the study found that one person on a team or crew held the information necessary to avoid an accident, but did not share that information because they assumed there was no need to communicate it.[26] The key word here is "assume." There is a paradox at work in SA because we all make decisions based upon assumptions. Our assumptions are informed through communication. And we communicate based upon what we often erroneously believe others need. Building good situational awareness, then, requires us to assume that others *do not know* the information we have rather than assuming that they do.

---

26   U.S. Coast Guard Research and Development Center. "Communications Problems in Marine Casualties." Report Number CG-D-21-00. October 2000.

The consequences of poor SA can be tragic as the events of July 1989 demonstrated. That month, the U.S. Navy was patrolling the Persian Gulf to prevent Iranian attacks on international shipping. In the two years before, Iran had attacked the U.S.S. Stark killing 37 sailors. The U.S.S. Samuel B. Roberts had struck an Iranian mine the previous year. And, in May of 1989, the U.S. had sunk an Iranian frigate. The situation was tense. The U.S.S. Vincennes, patrolling the Straits of Hormuz, mistook an Iranian passenger plane for an attacking fighter and shot it down killing 290 passengers and crew. The tragedy launched a seven-year research project called *Tactical Decision-Making Under Stress* (TADMUS) to understand how to train teams to make better decisions. The results of the TADMUS study are instructive to anyone leading a team in a high-stress environment. The Vincennes incident identified poor and incorrect information sharing at the root of bad decision-making. But, taken holistically, TADMUS exposed the need for teams to not just communicate better, but to establish mutual support (guideline *L7*) and debrief frequently as a team (guideline *E2*). In sum, it instructed teams to train and operate according to the basic Flawless Execution Cycle of plan-brief-execute-debrief (*Appendix A*) with an emphasis on briefing and debriefing.[27]

Strong SA rests on a foundation of multiple elements. First, team members must have a clear understanding of the task at hand and how that task aligns toward a much broader strategic and long-range vision of the future. As Simon Sinek has famously demonstrated in his bestseller, *Start With Why*, everyone on the team should feel connected to purpose, the 'why' they are doing whatever it is they are doing. Knowing the 'why' not only engages members of the team, but also identifies ultimate goals so that, in the face of unforeseen challenges and disruptions, individuals and teams may adapt and align their efforts to achieve that goal.

---

27   Cannon-Bowers, Janis A. and Eduardo Salas, Editors. Making Decisions Under Stress. (American Psychological Association, 1998).

Second, everyone on the team should know what their role(s) or task(s) is/are as it relates to the objective and long-range vision. Furthermore, each team member should know what the task(s) or role(s) are for everyone else on the team. Each team member should know what their fellow teammates are responsible or accountable to do. Without this knowledge, individual team members will not know to whom to pass information when it is discovered. In spite of how well-planned any task or project may be, it is always possible that critical new information may be discovered that fundamentally changes the assumptions made during the planning phase. When roles and responsibilities are unclear or hidden, information sharing is disrupted. To complicate matters, the leader of the team may not be able to serve as a central communication hub to distribute information in times of stress and when reaction times are critical to success. Certainly, the leader should always be informed when possible, but the leader may not necessarily be the most appropriate individual to take action when time is short or the volume of information is overwhelming. High-performing teams clearly understand with whom and when to share information. In most cases, actions and execution should be distributed across the team rather than centrally controlled.

Third, high-performing teams have rules of engagement or other decision-making rule sets that provide an appropriate level of autonomy. Good leaders give their teams guidelines and the latitude to make decisions on their own. Guideline *L6 - Delegate and trust*, addresses why this is so important. These guidelines tell teams under what circumstances and within what criteria individuals can make decisions on their own. Again, leaders may not have the capacity or time to make every decision or approve every action during the execution of a task or project. Decisions must often be delegated as a matter of necessity. Situational awareness, then, is essential to every team member so that they can exercise judgment appropriately.

Situational awareness concerns the active sharing of knowledge to better inform action. "After all," write Wharton and INSEAD professors Martine Haas and Mark Mortensen, "shared knowledge is the cornerstone of effective collaboration; it gives a group a frame of reference, allows the group to interpret situations and decisions correctly, helps people understand one another better, and greatly increases efficiency."[28] Research has also demonstrated that team members that discuss the relevant knowledge they bring to a task before planning and making decisions outperform other groups.[29] The world is too complex and volatile for information to be complete when plans are made and execution of those plans initiated. Teams and organizations must adapt or respond appropriately as new information and learning is discovered. It follows, then, that leaders must cultivate a high level of situational awareness among their team.

There is one final, critical point to be made about situational awareness. It is not just tactical, but also strategic. Day-to-day operations, the tactical execution of plans, requires a high level of SA. To strategy however, SA is even more critical. Organizations must be agile and capable of pivoting quickly when markets change. Strategic-level leaders must continuously update their mental model of the world, always testing their assumptions about their environment and evaluating the appropriateness of their strategy. Good SA isn't just about the little things, but the big things, too.

SWOT analysis is a well-known and widely used tool for developing strategic level SA. Simply, planners evaluate their environment in four areas—strengths, weaknesses, opportunities and threats. Management scholars have criticized SWOT not so much for its usefulness as for its relevance over time. SWOT is a good tool for developing

---

28 Haas, Martine and Mark Mortensen. "The Secrets of Great Teamwork." *Harvard Business Review*. (June 2016). Pg. 74.
29 Bonner, Bryan L. and Alexander Bolinger. "Bring Out the Best in Your Team." *Harvard Business Review*. (September 2014). Pg. 26.

SA initially, but once developed it usually gets put away and is never refreshed or validated over time. That's a fair criticism of any SA development tool. SA is a continuous process that must be maintained. The Flawless Execution *Stealth debriefing* process (*Appendix A*) is an excellent tool that provides regular inputs to refresh SA.

ACTIONS:

Share intentionally. Our workdays can be a storm of activity. Take a moment at the end of the day to take inventory of important news and informational items that the team should know. Share them during an appropriate meeting such as the next action item, a standup.

Hold a Standup. In this author's days aboard ships in the U.S. Navy we called it "O-call" or "morning quarters." Some organizations call it a "huddle". There aren't a lot of formal rules for such meetings, but the central idea is simple - to get everyone together at the beginning of the work day, run down the important events of the day, and give everyone an opportunity to inform the team about what their primary tasks or projects are for the day. That simple act alone increases SA exponentially in a team. But, what's more, it exposes opportunities for mutual support which will be addressed shortly in guideline *L7*. For leaders, it is a great opportunity to pass on thanks and other verbal recognition (guideline *L8*). Take care, however, that your standup doesn't last long. Set a target of no more than about fifteen minutes.

Train SA. As a leader, you are a coach. Ensure that you are helping your team identify shareable knowledge, underscoring the importance of sharing that knowledge and, critically, modelling (guideline *L3*) the appropriate way to share knowledge.

Debrief at all levels. Debrief a day's work for small teams. Debrief projects. Debrief strategic plans and the strategy-as-a-whole. The significance of debriefing for leaders and their teams is treated in greater detail in guideline *E2*.

Pick People's Brains. Schedule meetings with your direct reports on a regular basis. Make these meetings part of your *execution rhythm*[SM] (*O6*). This is an important leadership tactic that is useful wherever you fall in an organization's hierarchy. Some CEOs have such meetings every few months and spend as much as a half-day with direct reports and other key people to discuss what's new and what's going on in the world.[30] Have an agenda of questions and topics to discuss, but let conversations flow naturally. Actively listen during these sessions in accordance with guideline *C5*.

L5 – Facilitate Collaboration

> *"Individual intelligence, personality, skill, and everything else together mattered less than the pattern of idea flow. This is how kindergarteners beat educated professionals in building spaghetti towers with marshmallows!"*
>
> – Alex Pentland

Leaders are often poisonous to effective team collaboration. That's because most leaders don't know when to shut up. When leaders tell their team what they think, the team aligns to that thinking both consciously and unconsciously. That's why this guideline reads "facilitate collaboration" rather than "lead collaboration." Leading collaboration suggests taking control of it. Instead, leaders must understand how to facilitate teams in a manner that creates the best solutions from the knowledge and experience of the whole team.

---

[30] Charan, Ram. "You Can't Be a Wimp, Make the Tough Calls." *Harvard Business Review*. (November, 2013). Pg. 75.

"To err is human." If you were to go to Wikipedia and search for 'list of cognitive biases' you will find as many as 200 that have been identified in cognitive psychology and neuroscience. Leaders should care about cognition because being aware of these errors is the first step to avoiding them. Although there are hundreds of cognitive errors, there are a few that leaders should be especially careful to avoid. First, there are the individual errors humans are prone to.[31]

Overconfidence – Our mind likes to jump quickly to conclusions that arise from familiar patterns. We see a problem and, because it *seems* familiar, we instinctively blurt out an answer without careful thought. Then, we become stubbornly certain we are right and don't want to listen to contrarian viewpoints or evidence.

Framing Effects – The way in which information is presented to us, regardless of its coherence and logic, evokes emotions that affect our judgment. How a problem is presented to us - how it is framed - directly impacts the decision we make. It's like the old saw about first impressions. How we initially encounter something deeply affects how we continue to characterize that thing regardless of the facts or further experience. Framing effects linger.

Base Rate Neglect – Base Rate Neglect is one of the most pernicious sources of bad decisions in business. It's simply ignoring available statistics and established probabilities in favor of more immediate impressions and transitory data usually because quick emotional attitudes or responses get in the way of clear thinking and careful analysis.

Sunk Cost Effect – Also known as the *escalation of commitment effect*, sunk cost is an expensive and potentially destructive error. Sunk cost is a failure to recognize that what is past is unrecoverable such as spending a lot of money on a project only to discover that more and more is needed rather than cutting your losses and walking away from what might be endless cost overruns that can never be recovered.

---

31   Kahneman, Daniel. *Thinking, Fast and Slow*. (Random House, 2011).

Anchoring Effect – This one is especially dangerous in the planning process because it 'anchors' or establishes an argument or planning session around the first piece of information that is shared or discovered which is often an arbitrary or erroneous point. As leaders, we must be careful what we say and the initial information we share when facilitating planning or asking for input. This is a good reason why leaders and everyone else should keep quiet when initially generating ideas.

Similar to the general cognitive errors and biases above, there are some myths about performance that need to be addressed so that leaders can avoid them.

Ego Depletion – The brain is the most energy intensive organ in the human body. On average, it consumes about 20% of our total caloric intake, daily. So, it should come as no surprise that the more focused thinking one does, the more quickly the brain becomes fatigued. When it becomes fatigued, not only does it lose some of its capability for clear thought, it loses willpower. We become more susceptible to suggestion and our ability to resist our impulses lessens. So, working long, exhaustive hours may be counterproductive.

Context Switching – Do you believe that you are a good multi-tasker? Research into cognitive function strongly demonstrates that performing more than one thoughtful task at a time is all but impossible. Imagine trying to compose an e-mail while holding a conversation in a meeting. You may appear to be doing two things simultaneously, but what you are actually doing is switching rapidly between two different cognitive tasks. Switching between tasks has a cost both in time and in accuracy or quality.

There are cognitive errors and biases that transcend the individual and appear only in groups or teams. Here are some of the most prominent:

Groupthink – Identified in the 1960's, Groupthink was cited as the fundamental cognitive bias that led to the Kennedy administration's Bay of Pigs fiasco. Groupthink is a bad decision that is made by a team when debate between diverse viewpoints is squelched in favor of harmonious alignment. It's particularly prevalent when the leader of that team offers an opinion first and others agree with it to please that leader. It's important to note that following the Bay of Pigs disaster, President Kennedy learned from his failure and undertook rigorous critical thinking processes and debate within his cabinet to resolve the potentially catastrophic Cuban Missile Crisis shortly afterward.

Cascade Effect – A cascade effect is a specific form of a framing effect. Research has proven that in binary selections like a 'thumbs up' or 'thumbs down' option that one commonly sees in social media and rating systems is heavily biased toward whatever the first selection or vote happens to be. So, if the first person publicly votes thumbs down, then succeeding voters will have a significant bias toward voting thumbs down as well. The initial opinion tends to cascade to others. What's worse is that the cascade effect is more pronounced in small teams where the first opinion shared can quickly develop into *groupthink*.

Polarization Effect – Worse than the *cascade effect* is a frightening group error known as the polarization effect. Often, groups may begin a discussion with a moderate opinion one way or another, but after deliberation, actually adopt a radical or fanatical opinion that no one shared before. It's as though cascade effects snowball into *groupthink* which then evolves into an extremist ideology. The polarization effect is the echo chamber run amok where voices align and become louder and louder over time until no other opinion can be shared or discussed. As Canadian author and scholar Robertson Davies has pointed out, "Fanaticism is overcompensation for doubt."

Common Knowledge Effect (also known as the *hidden profiles effect*) – The common knowledge effect is an error in which the knowledge or information held by all the participants overwhelms the critical, but specialized information held by one or a few. Whether through fear of sharing unpopular or challenging information or because a loud majority drowns out a quiet minority, hidden information must be brought into group discussion so that it can be properly vetted and included in decisions and plans. Fundamentally, the common knowledge effect manifests itself as poor situational awareness that can drive bad decisions and actions.

Now for the good news. All these cognitive errors and biases can be either avoided or mitigated through good facilitation techniques and leadership behaviors. Facilitation techniques are covered in detail in the planning and *Teamstorming*^{SM} processes of Flawless Execution. Below, however, are the important actions that leaders can take to more effectively lead collaborative efforts.

ACTIONS:

Leaders speak last. The most a leader should do when initiating a collaborative session with his or her team is to clearly state the challenge or objective within context so that the team can solve it.[32] For a leader, it is dangerous to offer an opinion or suggest a solution before the team has had an opportunity to address it collaboratively. As a leader, reserve your opinion during debate. Listen carefully and facilitate your team toward a decision without affecting it unduly. But remember, you are the leader and when collaborative agreement cannot be reached, you must make the final decision.

Individuals think first. Allow individuals to form their own opinions before sharing with anyone else. A good way to do this is by using the *1-2-4-All* rule. Give everyone time to think about an objective or any one of the steps in the planning process by themselves—that is the "1".

---

32   Pietersen, Willie. *Strategic Learning* (Wiley, 2010) pg. 163.

Then, allow them to share their ideas with just one member of the team and to conclude a list of items as a pair—that is the "2". Next, bring the pairs together into teams of 4 and have them generate their decision or list of items—that is the "4". Finally, bring the whole team together for a final list, decision, or course of action. Some research demonstrates that teams that start problem-solving silently have as much as *twice* as much success in finding a solution.[33]

Think Ahead. Consider providing the topic, problem, or objective the day before you come together as a team to build a plan or make a decision. Give people time to think overnight. Research shows that the brain is more creative and thorough in its processing of ideas if it has time to unconsciously process ideas during distracted, relaxed or otherwise unfocused periods. This can save a tremendous amount of time in the actual planning session while stimulating more diverse and critical thought.

Think early. Schedule planning and decision-making sessions at the beginning of the workday or after a significant break such as lunch. Staying nourished is also important to keep your brain alert. Your brain needs fuel just like the rest of your body. It is usually best to sleep on big decisions if you have the opportunity. Do the bulk of your thinking one day, then make a final decision early on the following day once your mind has had an opportunity to refresh and consider the issue more deeply.

Optimize size. Remember the "stay lean" action from Guideline *L2?* Consider establishing an optimally-sized and diverse team. We now know that teams that are too small can suffer from a lack of cognitive diversity while teams that are too large cannot effectively communicate and coordinate to plan and execute. The optimal size of a team is from five to nine individuals.

---

33 Fabritius, Friederike and Hans Hagemann. *The Leading Brain: Powerful Science-Based Strategies for Achieving Peak Performance*. (Tarcher Perigee, 2017) pg. 167.

Take Time for Pie. "I sense you're not embracing the concept here," says Agent Kay (Actor Josh Brolin) to Agent Jay (Actor Will Smith) in the film *Men in Black 3*, "pie don't work unless you let it." The two had been hot on the trail of clues left by the film's villain, but the duo was unable to put all the clues together and track him down. Agent Kay had convinced Agent Jay to stop and have a slice of pie at a nearby diner. Agent Jay is dismissive of Agent Kay's suggestion right up until he is struck by a blinding flash of insight that helps the two protagonists along their path to saving the world from destruction. Such flashes of insight are common experiences for many of us. We wrestle with problems in our minds until, at some point of distraction, the insight we seek surprises us when we least expect it. Modern neuroscience has begun to demonstrate the source of this mysterious insight. Our minds are constantly at work, even at a subconscious level, grinding away at problems until we experience a 'blinding flash' of insight. Make sure that you allow yourself and your team to take time for pie.

L6 – Delegate and Trust

> *"Trust means freeing people to do their jobs and to make decisions. It means knowing people want to do well and believing that they will."*
>
> – *Schmidt, Rosenberg, and Eagle: Trillion Dollar Coach*

If you could do it all yourself, you wouldn't need a team. But since you cannot, you must lead your team to get things done. It follows, then, that leaders must delegate tasks and projects to others. And, since leaders are not omniscient or omnipresent, they must trust the individuals on their team to accomplish the tasks they have been delegated. Delegation and trust go hand-in-hand.

What is the opposite of trust? Distrust. What is the cost of distrust in a team or organization? Like the air we breathe, it is as obvious as the nose on our face - ever present yet unnoticed. It is called bureaucracy. Governments are especially adept at creating work to overcome the dangers of distrust. Every company creates bureaucracy too—some more than others. Distrust creates what the prolific political philosopher Francis Fukuyama equates to a 'tax' on organizations and social institutions.

> "If people that have to work together in an enterprise trust one another because they are all operating according to a common set of ethical norms, doing business costs less. . . . By contrast, people who do not trust one another will end up cooperating only under a system of formal rules and regulations, which have to be negotiated, agreed to, litigated, and enforced, sometimes by coercive means. This legal apparatus, serving as a substitute for trust, entails what economists call 'transaction costs.' Widespread distrust in a society, in other words, imposes a kind of tax on all forms of economic activity, a tax that high-trust societies do not have to pay."[34]

The cost of distrust is tremendous. Unfortunately, professional managers often assume that it is a necessary evil. It is not. Stephen M. R. Covey makes the same point as Fukuyama, although for a more popular audience, in his best-seller *The Speed of Trust*. High trust organizations can eliminate the friction, the high tax of bureaucracy, with its paralytic rules and transaction costs, that high-trust organizations avoid. Trust acts as a lubricant in the engine of organizations allowing them to run smoothly and efficiently.[35]

---

34 Fukuyama, Francis. *Trust: The Social Virtues and the Creation of Prosperity*. (Free Press, 1995). Pg. 27.
35 Covey, Steven M. R. Covey. *The Speed of Trust: The One Thing that Changes Everything*. (Free Press, 2006).

Developing greater trust pays big dividends. James Kouzes and Barry Posner, authors of the classic leadership text *The Leadership Challenge* have highlighted the significance of trust in organizations and cited research that demonstrates high-trust organizations can outperform low-trust organizations by as much as 286 percent. "Simply put," write Kouzes and Posner, "the more people trust their leaders and their organizations, the more positive the outcomes—for everyone."[36]

When you have trust, you can delegate tasks more easily and eliminate the need to micromanage those you have delegated tasks to. Although you should hold others accountable to completing tasks successfully, when things do not turn out well, assess what happened (*E2*) so that lessons can be learned and knowledge and experience developed for future success. You cannot expect perfection from your team one hundred percent of the time, but you can hold your team accountable to always learn from failure. Failure may not be welcome, but it is inevitable from time to time. A leader must take responsibility when his or her team falls short, while holding each member accountable to improving in the future.

"You can delegate authority, but you cannot delegate responsibility." That was the mantra of my formal military leadership training from decades past. If I were asked what the single-most memorable principle of leadership that I have lived and worked with all my professional career, the answer would be this simple differentiation between authority and responsibility. You can ask or order someone to do something, but it remains the leader's responsibility that it be done and done correctly. Leaders cannot blame subordinates or followers when delegated activities fail to be accomplished. "Hey, I told them to do it, but they didn't - so don't blame me" is a statement no leader should ever make. Owning outcomes that are beyond your personal

---

36   Kouzes, James and Barry Posner. *The Leadership Challenge: How to Make Extraordinary Things Happen in Organizations, 5th Edition.* (Jossey-Bass, 2012). Pg. 219-220.

capacity to control is an old but great leadership principle. The connection between delegation, a necessity, and responsibility, a choice, is one leaders must make daily.

It is also useful to turn the relationship between leader and led around and look at responsibility from the perspective of the subordinate or follower. When you, the follower, know that if you fail it is your leader that will be held accountable more so than yourself, you feel a greater sense of responsibility to your leader. As always, it is a bond of trust. Unless you are otherwise motivated to undermine your leader, you will feel the added obligation to not fail the person that has trusted you with an important task. Your task has become bigger than yourself.

There is a classic tool used in the U.S. military academies and other officer training programs to demonstrate great followership and a positive, can-do attitude. It is a short essay originally published in 1889 entitled, *A Message to Garcia*. The author, Elbert Hubbard, wrote it to extol the rare virtue of initiative, of great followership. Hubbard cited an event during the Spanish American War in which President McKinley sought to open communications with an insurgent Cuban leader, Calixto Garcia whose whereabouts were unknown. First Lieutenant Andrew Rowan, an intelligence officer, was recommended to McKinley as the right man for the job. So, without further insight or instruction than "Take this message to Garcia," Rowan set off and accomplished the task. What follows is a portion of the opening text of Hubbard's essay:

> "The point I wish to make is this: McKinley gave Rowan a letter to be delivered to Garcia; Rowan took the letter and did not ask, 'Where is he at?' By the Eternal! there is a man whose form should be cast in deathless bronze and the statue placed in every college of the land. It is not book-learning young men need, nor instruction about this and that, but a stiffening of the vertebrae which will cause

them to be loyal to a trust, to act promptly, concentrate their energies: do the thing—'Carry a message to Garcia!'"

Among many things, *A Message to Garcia* demonstrates what will later be described as a *bias for action* in guideline *K1 – Take action*. It also demonstrates the importance of situational awareness, or lack thereof, which we have already explored in *L4 – Cultivate situational awareness*. But, it especially demonstrates the power and importance of trust in an endeavor of great danger and significance.

Trust, at its best, is a two-way street. Leaders must trust their followers to do the right thing and followers must trust their leaders to give them the right tasks. Opening that relationship up to collaboration and cooperation is a magic formula for ensuring that both ends of the bargain are upheld. Thus, the previous item, *L5 - Facilitate collaboration*, is closely connected to delegation and trust.

So, why can't managers just hand subordinates orders and monitor their performance quantitatively? What if managers installed cameras everywhere to record worker activity? Maybe they should require their employees to wear tracking devices to measure their output and movement? It is simple—it's been tried and doesn't work. Human beings need autonomy, among other things, to perform at their best. Human beings need a sense of agency and purpose—that they are in control of their destinies and that the work they do matters.[37] It is not a new discovery, believe it or not. In spite of much of the 20th century's management practices falling along the lines of control systems that treated people like cogs in an industrial machine, military leaders have long known the limitations of command and control. Giving people a challenge and then stepping back and allowing them to meet it according to their abilities and judgment, has been a bedrock principle

---

37 Pink, Daniel H. *Drive: The Surprising Truth About What Motivates Us.* (Riverhead Books, 2009) pg. 71.

of leadership for eons. There's just one catch: you, the leader, must ensure they are capable and properly equipped with both the resources and the systems to accomplish the task. The U.S. Army's *Leadership Field Manual* states it clearly. "People want direction. They want to be given challenging tasks, training in how to accomplish them, and the resources necessary to do them well. Then they want to be left alone to do the job."[38]

General George S. Patton memorably summarized this same idea when he said: "Don't tell people how to do things, tell them what to do and let them surprise you with the results." Patton is suggesting that the 'surprise' of results is that a team you lead may be more innovative and effective than you may be yourself. Like President McKinley entrusted a mission to Lieutenant Rowan, let them be free to solve the problem on their own and, if you are leading well, they will know they can always come to you for assistance and guidance. "The best executive is the one who has sense enough to pick good men to do what he wants done," wrote Theodore Roosevelt nearly a century ago, "and self-restraint enough to keep from meddling with them while they do it." 'Meddling,' to use Roosevelt's word, dissolves trust. A good leader realizes that a subordinate's failure to perform is the leader's fault. Perhaps the leader did not, to use Roosevelt's phrasing, "pick the right man," or train and equip him or her properly. Whatever the cause, leaders own the responsibility for their subordinate's success and failure.

Trust also develops better employee or workforce engagement. Why? Well, autonomy is one reason why. Another is that people want to experience success. They want to be able to own accomplishment. Managers can diminish that experience when they 'meddle.' Leaders should give individuals on their team an opportunity to accomplish something on their own, maybe not as grand an exploit as Lieutenant Rowan's in a *Message to Garcia*, but with a small thing at first and then

---

38 *The U.S. Army Leadership Field Manual*. The Center for Army Leadership. (McGraw Hill, 2004). Pg. 6.

on to larger things. This is a key concept in guideline *K4 – Train and develop*, as well. "Grow people's experience of competence," writes psychologist Ron Friedman, "and you will inevitably grow their engagement."[39]

Building trust means taking risks and giving individuals on your team tasks to accomplish. You must delegate at least a little to start building the autonomy people need in order to feel competent and develop bonds of trust. And, as the reciprocal levels of trust increase between leader and led, a virtuous cycle takes over. If individuals are inexperienced, start with small things that have low risk or impact for failure. Build the level of challenge over time.

ACTION:

Plan to small wins. There is really one primary activity that you, the leader, can perform to delegate effectively and build trust. It is a notion known as *small wins*. In the Flawless Execution methodology, it is known as a *mission orientation*. Small wins are limited, short-range projects or tasks that are challenging but achievable and directly aligned to more visionary or strategic goals. Delegate opportunities for small wins to individuals and smaller teams. Give them the autonomy to plan and execute on their own. Just give them support when needed and back them up when they encounter organizational resistance. Give them the *psychological safety* (discussed in much greater detail in *E2*) to fail and account for their failures. Thank and reward them for success (*L8*). Granted, this is a complex action to take as a leader, but the payoff can be immense.

---

[39] Friedman, Ron. The Best Place to Work: The Art and Science of Creating an Extraordinary Place to Work. (Tarcher Perigee, 2014) pg. 159.

L7 – Orchestrate Mutual Support

"Alone we can do so little, together we can do so much."

– Helen Keller

Mutual support isn't just a synonym for teamwork. There is more to it. And, leaders don't just nurture it, they orchestrate it. Building effective mutual support is challenging. It requires leaders to utilize many of the other items in this book in the categories of organization, communication, and discipline.

Society suffers deeply from a lack of mutual support. Bonds of community have dissolved in many organizations and in society at large. People become transitory members of one group, one company or team and then move on to another in the modern 'gig' economy. Many larger corporations utilize matrixed organization charts which confuse, complicate and diminish membership in a specific team. Too often, modern workers feel alienated and alone, bereft of meaningful belonging to a 'tribal' group. Even a good leader to whom they may report is challenged to provide meaningful membership in a team when work is spread thinly across multiple projects without clear prioritization and alignment of any one of them to a common organizational goal.

We humans are social animals. That's not a recent realization. Aristotle pointed out that basic fact of human nature thousands of years ago. Yet, only now is cognitive and human behavioral science beginning to demonstrate that fact empirically. It is time to pay attention to the importance of socialization and belonging in organizations. Leaders ignore it at their peril.

Mutual support is more like tribal behavior than mere teamwork. It grows from the reciprocity members feel obligated to provide, which when practiced regularly and appropriately, grows into a superior level of teamwork enjoyed by high-performing teams.[40] Mutual support places responsibility for the team or mission in the hands of each member. Rather than the mere cooperation that teamwork implies, mutual support is an active search to identify the needs of each member of the team. It is a vigilance for when others might need help even when they are not cognizant of it. Mutual support, at its best, takes on the attributes of a self-aware superorganism in which each team member recognizes the needs of the individual team members and the roles and requirements that each must fulfill to achieve the mission.

Few have described the basic tribal or communal nature of humans better than journalist Sebastian Junger, best known for his best-seller *The Perfect Storm*. His crystalline description of the communal nature of humans in his book *Tribe* underscores the need for belonging to elicit moral, cooperative behavior and triumph over dishonesty and disengagement. Junger needed to understand why soldiers with experience in the wars in Iraq and Afghanistan often returned home, suffered from traumatic stress disorders, and to relieve their suffering, desired to return to the experience of war and all its horror. How could that be? Simply, it is because soldiers often form close bonds of belonging and purpose with fellow soldiers in combat. They develop mutual support, a sense of deep caring and a willingness to sacrifice to protect each other. Like pre-historic humans, soldiers cannot get away with immoral behavior toward each other, among those of their 'tribe.' "Modern society, on the other hand," writes Junger, "is a sprawling and anonymous mess where people can get away with incredible levels of dishonesty without getting caught."[41] The lesson to leaders is simple – don't allow your team to become an anonymous mess. Nurture belonging.

---

40 Dyer, William G., W. Gibb Dyer, Jr., and Jeffrey H. Dyer. *Team Building: Proven Strategies for Improving Team Performance, 4th Edition*. (Jossey-Bass, 2007). Pg. 60.
41 Junger, Sebastian. *Tribe: On Homecoming and Belonging*. (Twelve, 2016). Pg. 28.

However, there is a troubling dark side to our tribal nature. You can go too far in creating a tribal identity and work at cross purposes of the larger organization's goals. That's what General Stanley McChrystal explores in his popularized concept and book, *A Team of Teams*. What McChrystal recognizes is that elite, high-performing military teams demonstrate extremely high levels of group cohesion and mutual support. But, beyond those teams were the 'others,' the 'them.' The paradox of tribal behavior is that although in-groups treat each other with respect and heroic self-sacrifice, they treat outgroups with contempt and even violence. As evidenced by human history, "we" often treat "them" as less-than human, an animal, beast or even a demon. It is a sad legacy. Of course, tribalism plays out in corporations all over the globe, hopefully to less violent extent, as it forms siloed structures of poor communication and unhealthy competitiveness from team to team within a larger organization.

So, highly matrixed organizations run the risk of disengagement and confused priorities, while organizations with cohesive teams and departments run the risk of misalignment and diagreement on organizational strategy and vision. McChrystal's solution, his *team of teams*, is extreme transparency and a system of liaisons that act as links between teams to share information, foster understanding, and improve cooperation. This approach helps preserve the positive aspects of tribal behavior while diminishing the negative. Just as roles create divisions between individuals on teams (*O2*), tribal behavior creates 'seams' between tribes. McChrystal calls these seams 'fault lines.'[42] These seams are the weak points of organizations where failures often occur especially as organizations grow their members. Mutual support is the idea that individuals on a team extend responsibility for team success across the seams between individuals—that my teammate's success is 'our' success. Further, mutual support extends a team's

---

42 McChrystal, Stanley. *Team of Teams: New Rules of Engagement for a Complex World*. (Portfolio Penguin, 2015). Pg 124.

responsibility across the seams between teams because another team's success is everyone's collective success.

Whether you are a leader of the C-suite as a CEO or the leader of the smallest operational team at the front lines of a business or organization, you lead a team of just a few direct reports. Those team members may, in turn, lead another team with members that are leaders of teams further down in the hierarchical organization and so forth. The point is that large organizations are organized as teams of teams (*L2*). That is because we humans have a limit to the number of people we can lead and influence directly. A company of 10,000 employees is an organization rather than a team. It is made up of many teams, not just one. Thus, across the seams, between individuals and teams, mutual support strengthens the organization.

In aviation, mutual support is also known as the "wingman" concept. It is a collection of principles that have proven to be highly effective in developing high-performing teams. Mutual support is less about an action item to perform on a checklist as it is a shared "mindfulness" present in each member of the team that helps focus on the mission objective and on the team as a whole. It comprises three simple, easy-to-remember concepts—the three A's: attitude, altitude, and aptitude.[43]

Attitude is about mindfulness of self, team and environment. It's a personal commitment to assisting your teammates in accomplishing the mission objective and maintaining the team's, and your own, situational awareness (*L4*). Having a personal commitment is easier said than done. In the 'actions' below, a particular technique to influence higher levels of team commitment will be addressed.

---

[43] In deference to Zig Ziglar's mantra, "Your attitude, not your aptitude, will determine your altitude," the use of alliteration in this guideline item is coincidental and carries an entirely different meaning.

The second "A" is Altitude. As with "Attitude," altitude is also an aviation analogy. For a pilot, what is the most dangerous thing to worry about? If you hit the ground, rather than land safely, it's game over. Having a high altitude provides several advantages – 1) you can see a larger perspective and, 2) if something goes wrong, you have more time to solve the problem before you hit the ground. The closer you are to the ground the less perspective you have on the big picture and the less time you have to respond to challenges.

This analogy vividly expresses two phenomena. First, when we become task saturated—that is when we feel that we have too much to do and too little time to do it - we become less effective. We can only respond to those issues that are immediately present or pose an urgent demand or imminent threat. Second, functioning at low altitude degrades SA. Following this analogy, when we are low to the ground we can't see as far. Our horizon is diminished. We need to gain altitude to get a better vantage point on the current "image of reality." Multiple management scholars have made note of the importance of perspective. Jim Collins, in *Great by Choice*, claims that great businesses have the ability to "zoom out" and "zoom in." By 'zooming' Collins is advising organizations to develop an ability to focus intently on very "close to the ground" tactical issues and to "climb high" and take in the big picture, sense changes in the environment, and direct execution from an enlightened perspective.[44] Similarly, Heifetz, Linsky, and Grashow in their work on *Adaptive Leadership* underscore the importance of changing perspective by "getting on the balcony" and away from the "dance floor" to gain this same sort of full-mission capability.[45]

Becoming task saturated at a low altitude is not uncommon. It is often unavoidable. It is tough, as an individual, to overcome task

---

[44] Collins, Jim and Morten T. Hansen. *Great by Choice*. (Harper Business, 2011) pg. 103.
[45] Heifetz, Grashow, and Linsky. *The Practice of Adaptive Leadership: The Tools and Tactics for Changing Your Organization and the World*. (Harvard Business Press, 2009). Pg. 107.

saturation and gain altitude. However, an individual is not a team. Remember that providing mutual support means that you and other teammates assume the responsibility to watch out for each other. If one team member is flying at low altitude and another at high altitude, then the higher altitude teammate has a responsibility to assist his or her wingman in gaining altitude—to assume some tasks or to support them in other useful ways. Later, when the roles are reversed, the favor is returned. The result is a team that performs at a higher level because it is functioning across the 'seams.'

Finally, there is aptitude. Aptitude is a warning. As with the other two "A's" aptitude is expressed in terms of a military aviation analogy. Have you ever heard the old saw, "There are old pilots, and there are bold pilots, but there are no old, bold pilots"? Well, that is not really true. Modern military aviators are a very cautious lot. They must be because of their high-risk working environment. However, research shows a curious phenomenon. Statistics demonstrate that pilots involved in accidents are not old, nor are they young. Instead, accidents more frequently involve pilots with 4 to 7 years of flight experience. Those are the pilots that are approaching the middle of their military flying career. What's up with that? Remember when you were a high school freshman? You were scared of your new environment—and, therefore, cautious. But after the first year, you got confident and cocky especially with a whole new group of freshmen that looked so young and clueless to pick on. You had become a sophomore. The word "sophomore" derives from ancient Greek and it translates as "wise fool." That is what is happening with the higher incident rates of mid-career pilots. They have become overconfident. Their "attitude" is no longer sufficient to make up for their lack of skill and experience.

In the fighter pilot world, these overconfident pilots are likely to have a minor accident or close call that, if they survive, forces them to re-evaluate their "attitude." They learn from their mistakes and begin to improve their "attitude" from there forward, decreasing accident rates.

Where in your organizations and on your teams might this aptitude issue be occurring? Where is the notional aptitude level below the level of skill and experience?

As a leader, you must be mindful of the dynamic interplay of team cooperation that must take place daily to achieve goals, objectives, strategy and vision. You must orchestrate mutual support through vigilance and intentional action so that the members of your team take up the responsibility for each other's success and develop a heightened sense of awareness that they feel empowered and trusted to act (*L6* and *K1*).

ACTIONS:

Walk Around. "Management by walking around" is an old but good tactic for leaders. Be present to your team. Just saying you have an open-door policy isn't enough. Leaders must get out and interact with their team, not just on business matters, but also as human beings. Get to know your team on a personal level. Trust is built through personal relationships. No one is loyal to a leather chair. Get out of your office frequently and walk around. Talk to people. Observe. Look for ways your team can help each other out.

Talk Across the Seams. As a leader, you must do two things:

1. Verbalize the value each member of the team contributes to the whole. You should take opportunities to do this during a daily standup (*L4*) but also during informal interactions with team members. Identify and explain how one team member might assist another and when that is appropriate.

2. Verbalize to your team the value other teams or functions outside your own bring to the organization and what challenges they face to members of your team and to other leaders. Reach across the seams to other leaders and learn

what they do and how they do it. Understand how you and your team can support or aid other teams and when that is appropriate. Don't play 'high school cafeteria' and sit with your clique. Reach out to other groups and teams within the organization during informal social opportunities.

Attitude Pledge: To help the individuals of a team achieve the mindfulness needed to exhibit strong mutual support, teams can adopt a short and simple attitude pledge. This pledge does not necessarily require everyone to stand up, raise their right hand and recite it at the beginning of every workday. Instead, leaders should cover it once with their teams and infrequently thereafter, make it reasonably conspicuous on bulletin boards or other appropriate common areas of display, and perhaps put it on working documents and forms or even clip boards. It should be present, but not overbearing. Current research in human behavior demonstrates that it can be shaped by some very simple, unobtrusive techniques like the attitude pledge. For instance, cheating is substantially reduced when test takers must sign an honor code, even when they know there is no means of enforcing it. Theft is substantially reduced when people are unobtrusively reminded of the Ten Commandments. The trick is to create an environment where people do not feel they are being forced into a particular behavior. Humans have a tendency to rebel against forced behaviors and comply with mere suggestions and reminders that appeal to their inner sense of justice and moral behavior. Hence, this pledge addresses some core beliefs—the value and dignity of individual human beings and an individual's obligation to be responsible for themselves and to look after the well-being of others.

As a simple example, an attitude pledge is three brief statements to help remind team members of their obligations. First, "I am mindful of my environment, myself and my team-mates." The deck of an aircraft carrier during flight operations is a busy, confusing and very dangerous place. Being mindful of your environment is fundamental to safety. A common maxim in dangerous military environments is: "Keep your head on a swivel." That means keep a close eye on everything happening around you. Watch what your team-mates are doing. Do they need help? Do you see something they may not?

If you do notice something different, what do you do? Do you ignore it? No. "I bear responsibility to inform others and take appropriate action." In other words, if I see or hear or read something that changes the current situation or could possibly change the current situation, I have an obligation to tell others and do something about it. High performing teams do not assume that others have noticed the same thing and that someone will take action to address it. Also, high-performing teammates call out to other teammates when they are in error. Leaders of missions in the U. S. Air Force have a short and simple way of putting it. After briefing a plan, the leader might say "Make sure you all let me know if you see me do anything dumb, different, or dangerous." And that goes for everyone on the team.

Finally, creating an environment where people feel safe to voice their opinions is critical to building the right team "attitude." "I value the observations and opinions of my teammates." We must not dismiss or ignore others when they have something to say. Every member of a team must feel safe to express their opinions and pass on information. We must respect our team-mates to respect the whole team and its mission.

L8 – Thank and Reward

> *"A soldier will fight long and hard for a piece of colored ribbon."*
>
> *– Napoleon Bonaparte*

How do you incentivize people to do a good job? How do you keep them motivated? It would be nice if incentivization were simple, but it's not. What motivates people is one of the biggest questions of leadership. There are no straightforward answers because human beings are complex. Getting them to 'do stuff,' especially stuff they don't particularly want to do, differs from person to person and within the context of their needs and values. Poor leaders believe that monetary compensation is a primary driver of engagement. It's not—or, at least, it shouldn't be. Money matters, but it only matters so much. Appreciating people's effort, in most cases, matters more.

Why doesn't money matter that much? It's because we humans have a notion that deeply affects our behavior. We have a sense of justice. We care most about our pay when we feel that we are not getting our fair share. When pay is perceived to be doled out in a just manner, it no longer functions as a powerful motivator or cause for disgruntlement. Getting a paycheck at a regular interval doesn't incentivize either because it becomes expected. It doesn't elicit the addictive dopamine hit that other rewards do. Monetary rewards can motivate, but tend to be short-lived because the litigious nature of our culture and laws encourages monetary matters to be handled privately whereas one of the principal guidelines of motivating people to perform well is in thanking and rewarding them publicly. More on that in the 'Actions' section below.

The best advice on monetary compensation is to pay people justly and well enough to remove it as an incentive. Take it "off the table" so that it doesn't complicate what really matters.[46] What matters more than money to engage and increase performance in the members of a team or organization? There are many factors, but one of the most significant is recognition. Others, such as organizational purpose or the reason "why" an organization exists that the best-selling author, Simon Sinek, has popularized, will be addressed in the "O" section of

---

46 Dalio, Ray. *Principles*. (Simon & Schuster, 2017). Pg. 416.

this book. This guideline, *Thank and Reward*, provides guidance and understanding for how best to recognize your team for their efforts, accomplishing goals, and exhibiting the values of the organization.

Recognition matters. One research team found that recognition, properly executed, could make a company three times more profitable as compared to companies with low recognition activity.[47] People just want to be appreciated for what they do and to feel that they contribute meaningfully to organizational goals and purposes they believe in. The best way for leaders to connect team members to a sense of belonging is by recognizing their efforts. It's tempting to address complicated brain chemistry, but it mostly boils down to a few important hormones in the brain. As Paul Zak, the founding director of the Center for Neuroeconomics Studies, claims, public recognition results in the brain releasing two of the most powerful hormones. If leaders follow the actions outlined below, ". . . you can harness the double whammy of oxytocin and dopamine co-release in the brain."[48]

So, how should leaders recognize? How should leaders thank and reward people for their work and engagement? There are guidelines leaders should follow to make the most of recognition efforts. However, what follows are just guidelines. There are almost always good reasons, dependent on context, to push beyond these guidelines. So, keeping in mind that good judgment matters, consider the following:[49]

---

47   Gostick, Adrian and Chester Elton. *The Best Team Wins: The New Science of High Performance*. (Simon and Schuster, 2018) pg. 42-3.
48   Zak, Paul. *Trust Factor: The Science of Creating High-Performance Companies*. (AMACOM, 2017). Pg. 36.
49   The guidelines presented here are summarized from a multitude of overlapping sources. The principal sources include: Friedman, Ron. *The Best Place to Work: The Art and Science of Creating an Extraordinary Workplace*. (Perigee, 2014).; Fabritius, Friederike and Hans Hagemann. *The Leading Brain: Powerful Science-Based Strategies for Achieving Peak Performance. (*Tarcher Perigee, 2017); Pink, Daniel, *Drive: The Surprising Truth About What Motivates Us*. (Riverhead Books, 2009); Gostick, Adrian and Chester Elton. *The Best Team Wins: The New Science of High Performance*. (Simon and Schuster, 2018); Zak, Paul. *Trust Factor: The Science of Creating High-Performance Companies*. (AMACOM, 2017).

ACTIONS:

Recognize the deed. Recognize the deed rather than the person. "Sally, you put together an outstanding sales proposal that was, according to the client, the best they had yet seen!" is much better than, "Sally you are awesome!" The former emphasizes what was done rather than who did it which inspires others to do the same. The message to teammates is to write a great sales proposal rather than "be awesome". One is more specific than the other and, therefore, more actionable. It would be even better to impart exactly what qualities made the sales proposal great so that others could learn from it (more on that in guideline E2). Other research has proven the same regarding critical feedback. When feedback is negative, criticize the action rather than the person. Consider the difference between "Sally, your sales proposal lacked evidence of clear ROI" and, "Sally, you perform poorly." The former is constructive, the latter injures self-esteem without any direction on how to improve.

Do it Publicly: Thank and reward people in front of others, especially other team members. There's an old mantra about rewards—*reward in public but punish in private*. It's good advice and generally true, but if there is a lot of 'punishment' taking place in private, there's probably something dysfunctional about the team or its leadership. If you need to provide critical feedback to a team-mate, then that's best handled privately. However, debriefing, an essential activity of high-performing teams, allows for criticism, usually self-identified, to be shared among teammates. Debriefing will be addressed in guideline *E2*. Authors Adrian Gostick and Chester Elton recommend the *STEP* method for giving public praise. STEP is an acronym to remind leaders to tell a *story* when you have brought the team *together*, while *emphasizing* the core values demonstrated, and to *personalize* the moment.[50] It's worth reflecting upon the quote from Napoleon Bonaparte that introduces

---

50 Gostick, Adrian and Chester Elton. *The Best Team Wins: The New Science of High Performance.* (Simon and Schuster, 2018) pg. 48.

this guideline above. Small gestures have big impact particularly when there is a physical artifact emotionally attached to it. Military culture recognizes deeds and effort by awarding medals and their associated 'colored ribbons.' These are literally small, inexpensive tokens that recipients can wear, place on a desk, or stash away in a curio cabinet. Such tokens can take many forms—coins, buttons, pins, trophy cups, plaques, and so forth. The options are virtually infinite.

Do it infrequently. As a common courtesy for simple acts of cooperation and kindness, saying "Thank you" cannot be overdone.[51] However, like getting a paycheck on a regular basis, getting thanked and rewarded routinely loses its emotional impact quickly. Infrequent and unexpected recognition is most powerful.[52] As a leader, you should be saying "thank you" for special effort to one or more people daily, but not always to the same person. Roughly, more tangible rewards should decrease in frequency as they increase in scope and impact while the publicity surrounding them should increase proportionally. Get that report when you expected it? Thank the person who wrote and delivered it right then. That's just common courtesy. Did a team member go out of their way to make sure a difficult customer was satisfied? Thank them in front of the rest of the team at tomorrow morning's standup (*L4*). Did the sales team close a big deal? Take the team to lunch. These are simple gestures that are meaningful and cost little or nothing.

Do it now. Thank and reward immediately or soon after the commission of the act to be recognized or when evidence of its success is obvious. If someone wrote a great sales proposal, recognize that immediately as a standalone event. A simple public thanks and a call-out to its quality is all that's needed. But, if the proposal results in a signed contract a month later, then that too is something to recognize on a scale appropriate to the accomplishment.

---

51   Coyle, Daniel. *The Culture Code*. (Bantam, 2018). Pg. 78.
52   Gostick, Adrian and Chester Elton. *The Best Team Wins: The New Science of High Performance*. (Simon and Schuster, 2018) pg. 48.

Do it justly. Remember that people expect justice. They trust you, the leader, to ensure that the team environment remains fair. So, if they perceive that one or more members of the team are receiving unmerited thanks and rewards, or that you are ignoring the efforts of others, then you are undermining the sense of fairness and justice that people expect. Often, this can be perceived as favoritism which erodes the high levels of trust that high-performing teams need.

Peers do it best. When you, the leader, thank and reward, that's great. However, peer-to-peer recognition is more powerful. Teammates recognizing other teammates for their efforts is evidence of a strong, mutually supportive team. As the leader, your job is to nurture or nudge per-to-peer recognition.

O - ORGANIZATION

*"You do not rise to the level of your goals.
You fall to the level of your systems."*

– *James Clear*

'**O**rganization' is a big word. For leaders, it might represent the company or association that they serve—which can be a really, really, big thing like the U.S. Army or Walmart. You can organize things or physical objects. People are physical objects, but they are a very special class of things with both subjective and objective value. So, organizing people isn't like organizing your desk. People and their interactions with other people are extraordinarily complex things. Organizing people well and effectively, is, ideally, the responsibility of leadership. This series of guidelines will focus, not on organizing things or people, but on information and decision-making. In other words, this section deals with organization as a verb, rather than as a noun. What should you do as a leader to improve decision-making, actions, and activity to achieve organizational goals?

Too often, leaders focus on goals rather than the systems they should build and nurture to achieve them. As author James Clear indicates in the quote above, goals are unachievable without a system to bring them into reality. Leaders should ask themselves what their system is. If the answer isn't clear, then leaders need to organize the activity of goal achievement rather than just aspire to something and hope the team achieves it. What follows are some of the fundamental guidelines of organizing a group to be successful.

01 – Develop and Execute Standards

> *". . . standards make things work."*
> – *International Standards Organization (ISO)*

Teams and organizations must have rules. Unfortunately, the word "rule" carries a negative connotation. Rules are viewed as rigid and uncompromising. A better word is "standard". Its meaning is more flexible and positive. This guideline addresses the critical need for standards while simultaneously addressing how standards vary in a spectrum from rigid rules to flexible guidelines. Knowing when to use which—hard rules or soft guidelines—is the job of a good leader.

Standards should provide an appropriate amount of guidance—no more and no less—than the circumstances or context warrants. Thus, good standards live in the *goldilocks zone*—neither too hot nor too cold, too restrictive nor too liberal, too detailed nor too ambiguous. Standards should be just right. Standards in the goldilocks zone do not limit creativity. Instead, they liberate creativity and innovation. Artists have reflected on the need for limitation in order to spark genius. It's the same in any organization. The old adage that necessity is the mother of invention reflects a similar truism. Given complete freedom, it is difficult to find a place to begin the creative or innovative process. Management scholars Donald Sull of MIT's Sloan School of Business and Kathleen Eisenhardt of Stanford point out this essential nature of rule-setting. "By constraining infinite possibilities," they write, "simple rules allow creativity to flourish, less from thinking outside the box and more from deciding how to draw the box in the first place."[53]

Many organizations have statements of values. Value statements are good places to start establishing guidelines that keep the whole organization focused and aligned. Think of values as the guiding principles of the organization—the things the organization always or never does. Organizational principles establish the rules of the game. These are the fundamental rules that leaders must personify and enforce. Guideline *L3 - Model appropriate behaviors* addresses why leaders should exemplify the values and fundamental principles or culture of the organization. Standards must be defined and communicated openly to leaders for them to model. Nordstrom's guiding principle for all employees is simple. The department store even refers to it as "Our one rule." It is to "Use good judgment in all situations." That is easier said than done, but it guides every associate to provide the world-class customer service that has made Nordstrom so successful.

Netflix takes a different approach. It establishes two types of what it calls "necessary" rules so that the number and scope of standards remain limited to the most important. Netflix's direction to its leaders is to establish rules only to 1) prevent irrevocable disaster; and 2) for moral, ethical, and legal issues.[54] Humans in formal organizations have an innate tendency to create rules for the sake of creating rules. We are a naturally bureaucratic species. It doesn't take long for rules to proliferate to the point of absurdity which can paralyze an organization into inactivity and eventual stagnation or death. Netflix calls this "rule creep." Establishing standards for standards themselves, as Netflix has done, is an important consideration to make before you start developing standards of your own.

---

53   Sull, Donald and Kathleen Eisenhardt. *Simple Rules: How to Thrive in a Complex World*. (Houghton Mifflin Harcourt, 2015). Pg. 78.
54   Netflix's "*Reference Guide on Our Freedom & Responsibility Culture*" comes in the form of a pdf slide deck that is easily searchable online. Many companies have used it as a guide to develop their own cultural standards.

Limitations on standards empower organizations to act with good judgment. However, there are reasons to have complicated and highly directive standards, too. Some environments may justify the establishment of detailed safety and quality standards. Aviation is an excellent example. There are myriad technical standards for operating domestic airlines. The U.S. Federal Aviation Administration (FAA) sets and enforces these standards. The result is the safest form of travel. In 2017, in spite of the inherently dangerous nature of flight, there were zero deaths on U.S. domestic airlines.[55] Are domestic aviation standards complicated, vast, and restrictive? Yes, but the results stand for themselves. So, standards are good when used the right way and for the right purposes.

Having standards that are too prescriptive, too procedural, or those that do not allow for adaptation to the context at hand can actually create defects and errors. We humans tend to create bureaucratic rules where none are needed. One modern management expert has called this tendency "organizational debt" for its drag on innovation and agility.[56] Furthermore, overly prescriptive standards remove agency—they turn people into machines. Often, when people are forced to follow a standard that is overly prescriptive and poorly adapted to a given context, they may execute that standard precisely as it is written with willful intent to sabotage the results.

Generally speaking, standards fall into three categories—*guidelines*, *instructions*, and *procedures*. Understanding these categories will help leaders formulate the right degree of control for the given context.

New or novel situations call for the least restrictive standards. Consider standards that help people navigate uncharted territory as *guidelines,* or to use a fancy technical word, *heuristics.* Guidelines usually provide the right direction, but not always. Guidelines require

---

55 Shepardson, David. "2017 Safest Year on Record for Commercial Passenger Air Travel." *Reuters.* January 1, 2018.
56 Dignan, Aaron. *Brave New Work.* (Portfolio Penguin, 2019). Pg. 28.

individuals and teams to exercise good judgment. So, as in Nordstrom's case, there is a simple guideline to direct the right behavior in the extremely uncertain context of customer needs, expectations and desires. To an outsider, "Use good judgment in all situations" is extremely ambiguous. But, remember guideline *L6 – Delegate and trust*? Nordstrom has made that principle part of its operational culture with its "one rule."

Moving toward greater specificity, there are *instructions*. Instructions inform members of the organization of best practices rather perfect practices. They guide generally positive outcomes, while allowing room for judgment. Instructions are often much more extensive and verbose than guidelines. They might inform how to deliver goods or services to a customer. Because every customer situation is different, instructions must always allow for variation in context. Users of instructions must adapt to the situation. Instructions may mandate actions by using words like *will* or *must*, but also use flexible language like *should* or *may*.

The final and most precise form of standards are procedures. Procedures are algorithmic formulations of how to do something that eliminate guesswork. They inform how exactly something should be done without variation. Procedures do not require the application of good judgment or human agency. In theory, a robot could do it. Procedures exist to either alleviate the need to think about how to do something or to ensure a quality outcome very time.

ACTIONS:

Few and Simple. You should have only as many standards as you need and no more. Furthermore, the standards that you need should be stated simply and directly so that there is no ambiguity of meaning. Develop instructions to govern best practices and derive checklists from them so that the critical actions of an instruction can be easily referenced.

Visible and accessible. Train everyone to relevant standards (*K4*). Then make those standards accessible to everyone in the organization that might need them. People cannot follow standards if they don't know what the standards are, or don't have access to them when they need them for reference. Furthermore, don't let old, outdated standards lie around. It's best to establish control over standards by creating a shared file in any one of a multitude of electronic document management solutions.

Execute to standards. Notice the use of the word "execute" rather than "enforce"? That's because leaders lead by example, first. They model the standards (*L3*). They also take responsibility to hold others accountable to standards. One of the unfortunate failures within organizations is *normal deviance*. It arises from the neglect of established processes and standards. An infamous example of normal deviance is that of the explosion of the Space Shuttle Challenger in 1986. Narrowly defined operating parameters for launch were allowed to grow well-beyond designed limits in launch after launch until the context—in this specific case the ambient temperature—far exceeded the original design. The result was a disaster that caused the death of seven astronauts. In her research into normal deviance, Diane Vaughn famously described this institutional error. She wrote that, "The unexpected became the expected became the accepted." In other words, the discipline (*D* series of guidelines) to abide by best practices or other established processes can degrade over time as members of an organization become comfortable with risk . . . until they run out of luck. Leaders must ensure standards are correct and that they are executed correctly. When standards are in error, refer to the following action item.

Validate and maintain. Standards may eventually become irrelevant, outmoded, or obsolete. That can be dangerous for an organization.

Standards should be continuously validated through practice (i.e. execute to standards above). Debriefing (*E2*) is a primary practice to ensure changes, corrections, or improvements to standards are identified and implemented. Every standard should be intentionally scheduled for a complete review on a periodic basis.

02 – Align roles to goals

> *"If a man knows not to which port he sails, no wind is favorable."*
>
> *- Seneca*

"I know that these people are the most talented and capable in their profession and that they are doing *great* things," said the senior executive looking over a sea of cubicles, "but I'm not sure they are doing the *right* things." It's a not-so-shocking reality across industries—people working diligently to some end, but is it the *right* end? Alignment of effort is one of the great crises of our age. Are people in your organization clear on their role and goals? Do those roles and goals align to the team and organizational mission, vision, and strategy? How does all the activity fit together to create success? If, as a leader, you cannot answer that within the scope of your responsibility, are you really fulfilling your role as a leader?

Think about how *mis*alignment arises in organizations. Misalignment is rarely an issue in small organizations and teams because everyone is fulfilling multiple roles and has a clear understanding of how important each task is within each role. The members of small organizations don't have layers of hierarchy to obscure what's important to everyone. Small organizations, especially start-up companies, can't afford wasted effort. As organizations grow, however, misalignment starts to creep in. Roles get compartmentalized. Standards unnecessarily proliferate. The purpose starts to fade as the multitudes, fragmented into functional silos, wall themselves off and focus on their assigned tasks and lose sight of their part in the bigger system. Matrixed organizations complicate matters further by cross-assigning people to multiple project teams without painting a clear vision of how the projects fit together to achieve long-range organizational goals. One survey of new hires established that more than a third failed to understand their new role on the first day and as much as half remained confused three months later.[57]

Whether you are leading at the top of a small organization or within a dense hierarchy in a much larger one, your responsibility is to align roles to goals. There are two important, intertwined, yet distinct responsibilities at play here. The first is alignment of roles and goals and the second is focus and prioritization of roles upon the right goals (*D1* and *D2*). You can align your team toward a goal. But if it isn't the right goal, you've led them in the wrong direction. On the other hand, if you have the right goals but fail to lead their effort to align with that goal, you've failed to organize them properly.

Alignment is a word that gets thrown around a lot. Its definition is simple. It means, as Fred Kofman succinctly puts it, "…that everyone is playing to help the team win, regardless of his or her local performance indicators."[58] You must have alignment before you can empower a team to execute.[59] Everyone on the team must understand how their role aligns with team goals. Then, the team must understand how its role supports departmental goals. The department must understand how its role aligns with the division goals. And the division or business unit must understand how its role supports corporate goals. That's

---

57   Gostick, Adrian and Chester Elton. *The Best Team Wins: The New Science of High Performance*. (Simon and Schuster, 2018). Pg. 105-6.
58   Koffman, Fred. *The Meaning Revolution*. (Currency, 2018). Pg. 74.
59   Senge, Peter. *The Fifth Discipline: The Art and Practice of the Learning Organization*. (Currency, 2006). Pg. 218.

alignment—everyone, across the entire enterprise, working together to achieve a coherent, shared goal or set of goals. The accomplishment of specific role tasks is secondary to shared goals.

Alignment assumes that there is a set of cascading organization goals. If the organization has not clearly defined purpose, vision, or strategy, then alignment is impossible. "To empower people in an unaligned organization can be counterproductive" writes Peter Senge, senior lecturer at MIT and author of *The Fifth Discipline*. "If people do not share a common vision," he continues, "and do not share common mental models about the business reality within which they operate, empowering people will only increase organizational stress and the burden of management to maintain coherence and direction."[60]

Time provides another critical dimension to alignment in terms of goal setting. Vision and strategy provide long term goals on the scale of years. But those big goals must be broken down to the much smaller, shorter-term goals that front-line teams can align and execute towards on a daily, weekly, and monthly basis. Every organization must have such a *fractal* or cascading planning and goal-setting structure in place. Only then can the role of each member be aligned to goals. That seems obvious, right?

Don't fool yourself. Actually, long-term goal setting is contrary to our nature. We are short-term focused creatures. Lacking the belonging and purpose of a tribal, paleolithic culture, evolution has bred homo sapiens to sacrifice the future for the present. This is all related to the near-epidemic manifestation of depression in modern society. As research published in the *Journal of Affective Disorders* has described, "…the economic and marketing forces of modern society have engineered an environment promoting decisions that maximize consumption at the long-term cost of well-being. In effect, humans have dragged a body with a long hominid history into an overfed, malnourished,

---

60 Ibid. Pg. 136.

sedentary, sunlight-deficient, sleep-deprived, competitive, inequitable, and socially-isolating environment with dire consequences."[61] What we desire now is contrary to what is good for us in the long term because immediate gratification satisfies urges based in brain chemistry. It is a struggle for humans to sacrifice short-term compulsions for long-term success. Organizations small and large simply amplify this short-term focus when not properly managed and led toward purposeful ends.

ACTIONS:

Define purpose, vision, and strategy. And do it in that order. For leaders to offset our primal urge to satisfy the short term at the expense of long-term goals, the purpose, vision, and strategy must be compelling. They must excite and engage the people so that successive layers of leadership can more readily align roles to goals. Sometimes roles are straightforward, but hard to connect to long-range strategy. That's because strategies are fundamentally change efforts that may not require every functional role in an organization to change in an appreciable way. Every company has an accounting function, but that function may remain constant despite the change the rest of the organization is pursuing. Leader's must connect functional roles to the organization's vision. In the end, even the janitor at NASA headquarters in 1968 was helping put a man on the moon. What's your organization's moonshot? How does every role help achieve it? Making those aligning explanations to your team is part of *your role* as a leader.

Set goals. Set goals for business units, divisions, departments, teams, and individuals that align to higher-level, long-range goals and objectives. Refer to the next guideline (*O3 - Measurements follow intent*) for how intent and measurements operate together. Generally, for short term goals, like small projects, intent is straight-forward and

---

[61] Hidaka, Brandon. "Depression is a Disease of Modernity." *Journal of Affective Disorders*. 2012. Pg. 140

measurements can be rolled into the statement of intent to create a clear and measurable formulation of a goal to be completed at a specific date. As you develop longer-range goals separate the intent from the measurements and allow measurements to follow intent. You probably need three to five balanced, objective measurements for each long-range or strategic goal. Furthermore, modern management wisdom and this author's experience suggests that there is a limit of only about three big, strategic-level goals that an organization can pursue successfully at the same time.

Define roles. Defining roles so that everyone understands their responsibilities is critical to high-performing teams. However, the individual's ultimate responsibility is not to fulfill their role, but to help the whole team win. That goes for the leader of the team as well. So, remember to talk across the seams (*L7*). In many organizations, roles will be fluid, changing from one context to another and based upon emerging needs and changing organizational structure. Role-definition emerges from planning and decision-making and good role assignment should arise from strong collaborative processes. Leaders who lead collaborative planning and decision-making find that people often volunteer, if not openly compete, to assume roles. Assigning roles, particularly temporary ones, without directly consulting your team should be avoided. Good practice for temporary teams is to not only have a team leader, but also a *champion*. A champion is someone that holds a more senior leadership position in the organizational hierarchy and is invested in the success of the team's goals. The champion doesn't have to have an active role on the team. Instead, they 'champion' the team's purpose and act to remove obstacles to success through their positional influence. They are advocates of success and a 'sounding board' that the team leader can approach for advice and counsel.

Post progress publicly. Post and keep progress toward goals updated regularly. Guideline *O6* describes the need for an *execution rhythm*[SM] which should be considered as a driving factor of when to update progress. Harvard professors Teresa Amabile and researcher Steven Kramer present compelling evidence that the experience of progress is the single most important component of a satisfying workday.[62] Making this progress public has also been demonstrated to drive 'remarkable' results according to Stanford professor Jeffrey Pfeffer.[63]

03 – Measurements follow Intent

> *"Sweet is the lore which Nature brings;*
> *Our meddling intellect*
> *Mis-shapes the beauteous forms of things—*
> *We murder to dissect."*
>
> – William Wordsworth, The Tables Turned

Intent is primary. Measurements are secondary. In other words, intent is the holistic and subjective description of what needs to be achieved. A measurement, however, is a singular and objective description of only a part of the whole. As a planning tool, both are important. Intent describes what we really want, but it is often ambiguous and difficult to describe succinctly. Intent doesn't always specify where to focus effective action. Measurements, on the other hand, provide specificity, but may drive actions that are contrary to intent.

The U.S. war in Vietnam was a tragic example of getting intent and measurements in the wrong order. The intent was easily expressed as "win the war." That seemed obvious to everyone from the President of the United States on down to the average citizen. The measurements of success, however, were not related to territory gained or surrender

---

62 Amabile, Teresa and Steven J. Kramer. "The Power of Small Wins." *Harvard Business Review*. (May, 2011).
63 Pfeffer, Jeffrey. *Leadership BS: Fixing Workplaces and Careers One Truth at a Time*. (Harper Business, 2015). Pg. 53.

by the enemy. The strategy was to exhaust the North Vietnamese ability to fight and the measure of success was straightforward—body count. That, of course, encouraged killing as many enemy forces as possible. In military history, it's known as a 'war of attrition,' a really awful thing. And, in a context in which enemy and ally were hard to differentiate, South Vietnamese ended up on the bottom line of the tally with their North Vietnamese foe. That turned allies into enemies, ultimately forcing the U.S. to withdraw and end the war as a loss—all because measurement got ahead of intent.

In business, the call center is a classic example of getting measurements ahead of intent. A business has a call center to handle customer orders, address issues, and otherwise serve customer needs. Commonly, call center associates are handed productivity goals in terms of speed of handling a call or number of calls per day measurements. Of course, those measurements incentivize call center associates to get off the phone with a customer as quickly as possible. The result? Poor customer service resulting in otherwise loyal customers walking away. Zappos, an online shoe sales company, upended that model by allowing (and even incentivizing) call center associates to spend as much time as they needed with a customer to ensure that they are fully satisfied. Zappos understood that short-sighted measurements like call time drove down customer satisfaction. They reversed it and have a legendarily loyal customer base.

When you thank, reward, or in some other way incentivize people to do something highly objective like keep an average call time under five minutes, make 30 widgets per hour, or see 25 patients per day, that's what you'll get because most people will do what is necessary to meet the standard (Guideline O1). If that objective measurement isn't all that you want, however, all that you *intend* to be done, then you have probably set up a counterproductive system that will only work against your intent.

Measurements can produce short-term thinking. Wall Street provides a great example. Investors want returns, usually in dividends on an annual basis. But a year in the life of a company that is pivoting in a volatile market and making an investment in a multi-year strategy may need time to retrench. If that company is pressured to return shareholder value on an annual basis, there may be no future. The same holds true for incentivizing teams and individuals. As Daniel Pink has observed, "…carrots and sticks can promote bad behavior, create addiction, and encourage short-term thinking at the expense of the long view."[64]

As this book goes to print, one of the best-selling business books is *Measure What Matters* by John Doerr. One of the core messages of the book, an idea tested in some of the world's most successful companies, is that you must first determine what you are trying to achieve and then isolate the measurements to focus on what will directly achieve that goal. And critically, if the measurements drive the wrong results, then you must be willing to abandon them in favor of another measurement.[65] The implicit warning here is that if you set up an annual measurement and tie it to annual incentives or bonuses—and that measurement drives the wrong results—then you have to change it quickly. Many companies get caught in this trap and wait too long to pivot away from poor measurements.

For these reasons, many companies such as Netflix are abandoning annual objectives and their corresponding metrics—not just because they might drive the wrong behaviors, but because the speed of change makes planning annual incentives challenging.[66] The strategic

---

[64] Pink, Daniel. *Drive: The Surprising Truth About What Motivates Us.* (Riverhead Books, 2009). Pg. 47-49.
[65] Doerr, John. *Measure What Matters: How Google, Bono, and the Gates Foundation Rock the World with OKRs.* (Portfolio/Penguin, 2018.)
[66] Charan, Barton, and Carey. *Talent Wins.* (Harvard Business Review Press, 2018). Pg. 116.

planning horizon for most industries is shrinking. For some, a year can seem like an eternity.

The key point of this guideline is to understand that intent supersedes measurement and, when constructed appropriately, intent is more resilient than measurements. Measurements drive results, but they should always take a supporting role to intent. As a simple example, intent might be phrased as "Provide the best possible customer service." Measurements that support that intent might be that customer hold times average less than 15 seconds and net promoter scores (NPS) are greater than 8.2. The intent is the whole. Measurements are the parts. Intent is often subjective, hard to put into words and challenging to be precise. Measurements complement intent by providing objectivity and precision. Both are needed because in any complex environment context matters. We recruit people into our organizations to make decisions. Decisions require judgment—good judgment. Measurements often shut out judgment for blind obedience to a number. Intent encourages people to exercise good judgment—what they were recruited for in the first place—in spite of those numbers. When leaders hold people accountable to intent before the measure, they win.

What's more, intent and measurements are often framed more appropriately and effectively when the people that are held accountable to achieve them are part of the process of framing them. Build intent and supporting measurements collaboratively with your team (*L5*).[67] They'll understand better what needs to be accomplished and why. Furthermore, they'll be better able to exercise judgment and take appropriate action that might even run counter to the established measurements.

---

67   Pink, Daniel. Drive: The Surprising Truth About What Motivates Us. (Riverhead Books, 2009). Pg. 47-49.

ACTIONS:

Describe intent first. Describe your strategic and long-range goals subjectively as *intent*. Try to leave numbers and other objective statements out of descriptions of intent. Articulating intent can be challenging. So, invite the team to collaborate and share ideas on how best to describe the intent in a language everyone agrees upon and understands.

Determine measurements, second. After you have framed your intent, carefully consider several ways to measure whether you have or have not been successful in achieving your intent. Again, involve the team in doing this. When individuals have a role in establishing their own goals, they will be more engaged to succeed in accomplishing them. Over time, track the measurements and periodically ask yourself and your team if the measurements are driving the right actions to achieve the intent (*E2*). If not, change the measurements immediately.

04 – Establish a Course of Action

"If you are not confused, you don't know what is going on."

– *Jack Welch*

Having a bias for action, an idea explored later in guideline *K1*, is usually the best advice for leaders in a volatile, rapidly changing world. But, acting presupposes that a decision or plan has been made via a rational, well-thought-out process and good judgment. So, it's worth considering what the word *judgment* stands for—not what it means literally—but, what it *is* and its limitations. It's worth reflecting on what leadership scholars Noel M. Tichy and Warren G. Bennis write in their excellent exploration of the subject in *Judgment: How Winning Leaders Make Great Calls*.

> *"Judgment is too complex a phenomenon, too dependent on luck and the vicissitudes of history, too influenced by personal style and countless other variables, to pin it down once and for all. Doubly-doomed is the hope of creating an elegant theory of judgment. Whenever anyone comes close to formulating a final word about judgment, some unforeseen, history-changing event rewrites all that preceded it."*[68]

A leader's capacity for good judgment is founded on their knowledge and experience which will be explored in greater detail later. It does not arise from reading a single book or holding a single job. It arises from reading and studying an immense library that can never be fully consumed intellectually and from a lifetime of effort and struggle in a multitude of fields from battlefield to boardroom and everywhere in between. Everyone exercises judgment—most poorly, a few well, and none perfectly. Thus, pooling intellectual and experiential resources is critical to establishing good judgment in a team. Decisions should be informed by collective good judgment rather from the judgment of the leader alone. However, the leader is ultimately responsible for the outcome. The decision or course of action they choose is *their* choice. Good leaders make informed decisions, but a leader must ultimately exercise their judgment over that of the team when opinions differ. That is the burden of leadership. As the introductory quote above from Jack Welch suggests, people who are certain about things should be looked upon with suspicion.[69] No one really knows what's going on or what's going to happen at the deepest, most complex level of reality.

Making a decision or developing a course of action is a *best guess*. That's all. It isn't guaranteed to be the right decision or the best course of action. Thus, the following *K* and *E* series of guidelines is critical

---

[68] Tichy, Noel M. and Warren G. Bennis. *Judgment: How Winning Leaders Make Great Calls.* (Portfolio, 2007). Pg. 4-5.
[69] Tichy, Noel M. and Warren G. Bennis. Judgment: How Winning Leaders Make Great Calls. (Portfolio, 2007). Pg. 71.

to reaching *confident* decisions and courses of action. A decision is a single act to pursue (or not to pursue) a course of action. It may be binary—a *yes* or a *no*. A course of action is a list of actions or activities that need to take place to achieve an objective—a plan. Some decisions don't require plans, but all plans require a decision of whether or not to pursue a specified objective. Thus, planning is a decision-making process as much as it is a course-of-action-creating process. A good planning process is rational, inclusive of the knowledge and experience of a diverse team, and helps the team and its leader to conclude whether or not to pursue its objective. Time is usually of the essence when making decisions and developing plans. As a team activity, leaders should gather as much diversity of ideas and opinions as possible in a short amount of time.[70] Later, guideline *K1 - Take action* will address why time is such a critical issue. The planning and decision-making process is also a critical element to success. A 2010 McKinsey study demonstrated that good processes are six times more valuable than good analysis![71] This is not to say that analysis is not important. Garbage in is garbage out. But if the process isn't a good one, it doesn't matter what goes in, garbage is almost certain to come out.

Beyond simple decisions to pursue one course rather than another, it's important to reflect upon the *goldilocks principle* introduced in guideline *O1* as it pertains to creating detailed courses of action such as project plans. Leaders tend to over-prescribe or over-plan the tasks or activities of a project. In VUCA environments, too much detail creates fragility in plans. Things almost never go as planned. So, over-directing the details, much like micro-managing daily operations, only sets teams up to fail. Courses of action, therefore, should not include the "breathing steps" – all the details of what must be done down to when the coffee breaks are taken and

---

70   Edmondson, Amy. *Teaming: How Organizations Learn, Innovate, and Compete in the Knowledge Economy*. (Jossey-Bass, 2012). Pg. 246.
71   Lovallo, Dan and Olivier Sibony. "The Case for Behavioral Strategy." *McKinsey Quarterly*, March 2010.

the wrenches turned. Complexity demands flexibility. Teams need to adapt on the fly—to adjust their approach and often act in unexpected ways that could not be foreseen around the planning table. They also must respect the human agency. When people are merely following a pre-programmed routine like robots, they disengage. People do their best when challenged to exercise their intellect, skills, and judgment. This simple idea was explored in guideline *L6*, delegate and trust. Thus, like the goldilocks principle, good plans are neither too directive nor too unclear. Instead they provide just the right level of guidance and structure.

ACTIONS:

Utilize a rational process. The *Flawless Execution* six-step planning process provides detailed guidance to develop objectives, decisions, and courses of action. *Appendix A* provides additional guidance. The process is summarized as follows:

- Step 1: Develop a clear, measurable, achievable and aligned objective.
- Step 2: Identify the threats or obstacles that stand in the way of achieving the objective.
- Step 3: Identify the resources available or needed to achieve the objective.
- Step 4: Evaluate lessons learned from previous experiences.
- Step 5: Develop a course of action indicating *who*, will do *what* and *when*.
- Step 6: Plan for contingencies by determining what will trigger a contingent action and the initial actions that will be taken when triggered (*O5*).

05 – Plan for Contingencies

"The test of a first-rate intelligence is the ability to hold two opposed ideas in mind at the same time and still retain the ability to function."

– F. Scott Fitzgerald

Leaders must balance two opposing attitudes: the confidence that they, and their team, will succeed while simultaneously assuming they will not. Certainty is arrogance. The best laid plans are only guesswork. So, making decisions and developing plans requires leaders to consider what could go wrong and what to do about it if it does. Furthermore, planning for contingencies, helps keep you proactive rather than reactive.

Leaders rarely face do-or-die scenarios. Unlike Alexander the Great and Hernan Cortez, who burned their ships when invading distant lands to encourage their troops in an all-or-nothing bid to win, good leaders have a back-up plan. Beware those who suggest otherwise. A recent case in point is Elizabeth Holmes, the founder and CEO of Theranos. "I think that the minute that you have a backup plan," said Holmes in 2015, "you've admitted that you're not going to succeed." Three years after making this foolish statement, Holmes was indicted for fraud and stepped down as CEO of Theranos. Her personal worth dropped from $4.5 billion in 2015 to zero just a year later.[72]

Having a positive attitude is unquestionably beneficial to teams and leaders. But, being irrationally optimistic is not. The difference is that of two mindsets—the *deliberative* and the *implemental*. It is not that one is better than the other, but that both should be utilized

---

72   Wood, Robert W. "Theranos Founder Elizabeth Holmes May Have Lost $4.5 Billion, But Gets No Tax Deduction." *Forbes.* June 6, 2016.

in sequence[73]. A deliberative mindset is a phase of thinking in which individuals and teams keep an open mind and evaluate whether an objective should be pursued. It includes identifying what could go wrong in pursuit of that objective and lists those as cons, threats, or obstacles to success. An implemental mindset, however, should be engaged *only* following the rational decision to pursue an objective. Research by Peter Gollwitzer and Ute Bayer demonstrate two important phenomena. First, "the deliberative mindset provides a window to realism…" The psychologists also note that it "…hampers action initiation and persistence…"[74] In other words, it can lead to hesitation or a phenomenon known as *analysis paralysis*. So, the deliberative mindset provides an ability to identify possible sources of failure and sets leaders and their teams up to address them in contingency plans. But, shifting to an implemental mindset can lead to over-committing to a course of action which may result in escalating cost and effort or even catastrophic failure. The key learning here is to identify potential sources for failure while individuals and teams are in the deliberative mindset and to address them with premeditated contingent actions. In short, plan for contingencies before shifting to an implemental mindset and executing a plan.

Murphy's Law is probably the most reliable principle for leaders: if something can go wrong—and it certainly can—it probably will. So, having a 'plan B' is more than just a good idea, it's an essential survival skill. The U.S. Army Special Forces understands this and employs a form or extreme contingency planning known as "PACE" planning. P.A.C.E. is an acronym that can be simply summed up. "P" is for plan; "A" is for alternate plan; "C" is for contingency plan; and "E" is for emergency plan. Most people or organizations don't need to

---

73   The Flawless Execution© planning process is designed to initiate planning deliberatively at first and then shift to an implemental mindset at an appropriate point.
74   Gollwitzer, Peter M. and Ute Bayer. "Deliberative versus Implemental Mindsets in the Control of Action." In S. Chaiken & Y. Trope (Eds.). *Dual-Process Theories in Social Psychology*. (Guilford Press, 1999). Pg. 403-422.

plan for contingencies to such an extreme, but the principle is valid in highly volatile situations such as combat. Remember what the Prussian General Helmuth Von Moltke famously said, "No plan survives first contact with the enemy."

So, contingency plans are really part of the plan or decision itself rather than something separate. That's a key point to keep in mind. Do not separate plans from contingencies. Remind your team of contingencies frequently. The more clearly the whole team understands the contingencies and their accompanying responsive actions, the more quickly they can be put into place. Both speed and certainty of response matter. Speed of response is intuitive—the more quickly you address an emerging contingency, the better. Certainty of response should also be intuitive, yet its importance often gets missed. Individuals often hesitate to respond. Teams are typically even more hesitant to respond due to the *bystander effect.* Also known as the *Genovese syndrome* for the murder of Kitty Genovese in 1964 in which as many as thirty-eight witnesses to the murder took no action to prevent it, the *bystander effect* is a group behavioral phenomenon in which the greater the number of bystanders, the less likely it is that any one of them will take action to help. It's simple to validate. When you see someone in need or in distress in a crowd, you think to yourself "Oh, with all these people, someone will help. I don't need to." The bystander effect is a dispersion of responsibility that is common in low-performing teams.

The reverse is also true. Some individuals and teams can become overly committed to a plan or objective and fall prey to the *sunk cost effect.* A sunk cost is a cost that has already been incurred and cannot be recovered. The cost may be considered in terms of capital, effort or other resources. These costs are in the past, beyond one's capacity to affect. In purely rational terms what is past and outside our control should not bear on the decisions we make that impact our future; yet they do. The sunk cost effect is to continue pursuing a course of action regardless of mounting resource commitments and costs, and a failure to achieve the results or effects expected. Emotionally, we consider the amount of effort we have dedicated to pursuing some goal and continue pursuing it because we do not want to admit that we have failed or made a poor decision to pursue the objective in the first place. We don't want our efforts to be spent in vain. Sunk cost is an overcommitment to an implemental mindset.

In business, the sunk cost effect can drive companies to continue to pursue hopeless projects rather than cut their losses and pursue more promising activities. These projects, however, do not always fail. It is not ultimately the success or failure that matters in the sunk cost effect. Instead it is the use of sunk cost reasoning that is the mark of the effect. For example, the development of the Concorde supersonic passenger jet and the BART service line to the Oakland International Airport were both defended by its developers and continued despite cost and time overruns. In the case of the Concorde, the venture limped along for decades and ultimately was terminated, having never been a profitable enterprise.

Keeping sunk cost in mind, when should a leader and their team abandon a course of action? Should an exit strategy or plan be put in place? A contingency plan might address things to stop doing or to discontinue as much as they might address actions to take. In either case, clear indicators or triggers need to be in place. When so many dollars or so much time has been spent without success, it's time to quit before more is wasted. Like a trip to Las Vegas, know how much money you are willing to lose at the blackjack table and take only that amount in cash with you. When its spent, you're going home.

ACTIONS:

What could go wrong? Planning for contingencies occurs at the end of, or immediately following, the determination of a course of action (*O4*). This is a deliberate step to review your course of action with a mind to identify the possible failures or events that might occur in pursuit of your objective. Reach back to the list of cons, threats or obstacles to success that you made during the deliberative portion of planning. Whenever possible, you should also conduct a *red team (E1)* of your plan to get additional, unbiased feedback to help identify potential issues that may have escaped you and your team's attention.

How will you know when it does? What are the unambiguous indications that a contingency is occurring and that you and your team need to take action *(K1)*? What's your budget or time limit before you abandon the course of action? What market indicators shift and compel you to change that new product strategy you've been pursuing? Think of these indicators as 'triggers.' Trigger is a good word that suggests action is contingent or caused by an event. These triggers should be communicated *(C3)* clearly and often *(O6)* to your team - and changed if necessary.

What will you do? When the contingency is triggered, what will you and your team do to respond? Think in terms of initial actions to respond to the contingency and, possibly, in terms of different or new plans that will be executed as a response. Most contingencies won't need fully developed plans. Rather, strong responses to contingencies may only be a few simple actions. However, emergency response plans may have to be detailed to contain or minimize damage created by major contingencies. Think about and write down the steps you will take in the calm of the planning phase rather than trying to determine a response in the stress and potential chaos of the execution phase.

O6 – Establish an Execution Rhythm[SM]

> *"Rhythm is deeply important to human beings. Its beat is heard in the thrumming of our blood and rooted in some*

of the deepest recesses of our brains. We're pattern seekers, driven to seek out rhythm in all aspects of our lives."[75]

– Jeff Sutherland

As standards organize the *how to*, a tempo or cadence organizes the *when to*. When will you and your team establish regular, efficient, and effective interactions while also giving everyone the time they need to accomplish their tasks and fulfill their roles?

Timing matters. Furthermore, rhythm matters. *When* we choose to do things as individuals matters because everyone has a peak performance time of the day, a trough where performance lags, and a rebound. However, natural cycles may be different from one individual to another. Some peak in the morning, most towards the middle of the day, and the remainder later in the afternoon or evening. You know this from life experience. There are morning people, evening people, and those that fall in the middle.

These varying peaks and troughs may create a challenge for leaders of teams with mixed composition. Beyond timing your own activities for best results, as a leader you will have to *sync*, to use a word chosen by Daniel Pink in his book *When: The Scientific Secrets of Perfect Timing,* to establish a cadence or tempo for your team.[76] From choruses to basketball teams, timing matters. And, timing needs to be top down—set by leadership. It's tough to synchronize from the bottom-up unless there is some external rhythm that provides a syncing opportunity such as train schedules. For most organizations though, syncing must be imposed by some authority within. That's why organizational hierarchy is important. The U.S. military has been practicing this basic idea for decades. It calls its syncing, *battle rhythm*.

---

75   Sutherland, Jeff. *Scrum: The Art of Doing Twice the Work in Half the Time.* (Crown Business, 2014). Pg. 85.
76   Pink, Daniel. *When: The Scientific Secrets of Perfect Timing.* (Riverhead Books, 2018).

But there's something more surprising about syncing to increase performance. Pink calls it the *Uh-oh Effect*. There is significant project team data that shows, regardless of composition and context, progress toward a goal lags until the mid-point between a project's start date and completion date. Once the team hits the midpoint, there is a recognition that the team must get busy making progress to achieve their goal on time. There appears to be a realization such as: "Uh-oh, we've got to get busy. We've wasted half our time!"[77] So, the question for leaders is how to create a cadence or tempo of team interaction to improve execution efficiency and accelerate performance.

Take two metronomes and place them at opposite ends of a room. Set them in motion and watch what happens. Both tick away in each other's own separate rhythm never aligning or getting in sync with each other. But, place both of those metronomes on a smaller, substantial but flexible platform, set the metronomes in unsynchronized motion, and watch what happens. Depending on the construction and composition of the platform, the two metronomes will naturally synchronize relatively quickly. Why is this? It is because the metronomes are transmitting subtle, aligning vibrations to each other through the platform. These vibrations interact to achieve a natural synchrony.

If you are wondering if the physics of two self-regulating metronomes is really related to complex human systems, there is strong evidence that suggests it is. In psychology, social conformity is one of the most basic and widely accepted phenomena. Individuals within a group tend to achieve conformance and harmony, much like the metronomes. Richard Daft, Professor at Vanderbilt University's Owen School of Management, advises his students to connect with others that demonstrate the behaviors they want to develop within themselves. For students that have trouble focusing on their studies, he suggests

---

77   Pink, Daniel. *When: The Scientific Secrets of Perfect Timing*. (Riverhead Books, 2018).

simply sitting near other students that are studying.[78] Professionals who work at home often opine about the loss of such influence. Some have difficulty focusing on work in a home environment. The office, however, helps workers focus more effectively simply because it's natural for humans to conform to the environment and the behaviors of those around them. Connectivity and proximity are important dynamics in human systems.

However, self-regulation is a double-edged sword. It means that it takes very little effort to synchronize the activities within an organization so long as there is a responsive medium (or process) that connects the various activities. That is the good news. The bad news is that if there is no responsive medium then the result is either asynchronous behavior between the various activities or, worse, synchronous behavior that is at cross-purposes with the organizational goals.

As Edgar Schein, a world-renowned scholar of organizational culture, has pointed out, culture is a phenomenon that operates below the surface, that it is "invisible and to a considerable degree unconscious."[79] Like the subtle vibrations that eventually synchronize the two metronomes, culture works behind the scenes, almost imperceptibly, to affect how the organization functions for good or ill. Just as the metronome provides guidance to a single musician or a group of musicians, simple coordination via a simple process provides the guidance to align an organization.

There is an oft used, worn out, and negative image of some organizations and their leaders. It is the familiar image of an oared ship propelled by many shackled slaves, bent over row upon row of oars. In unison, they pull to the beat of a task master's drum: stroke…stroke…stroke. If the oarsmen on either side of the ship pull to a different beat,

---

78   Daft, Richard. *The Executive and the Elephant: A Leader's Guide to Building Inner Excellence.* (Jossey-Bass, 2010). Pg. 108.
79   Schein, Edgar. *Organizational Culture and Leadership, 5th Edition.* (Jossey-Bass, 2016). Pg. 8.

what will happen? The ship will turn in the direction of the slower oarsmen. And, what will happen if the oarsmen pull at their own unregulated pace? Well, you may think that the effort of all those oarsmen will average out and keep the ship steering a steady course. Perhaps, but, if the oars are not moving in sync, they bump into each other. Without a coordinated rhythm, the interference of all those oarsmen rowing at their own pace may be disastrous.

For organizations to succeed, they must possess alignment—that is coordinated effort to achieve organizational goals. To illustrate the potentially disastrous consequences of misaligned effort, consider the following comments by Enron Capital and Trade Resources President, Kenneth Rice, as he describes his strategic approach to management scholar Gary Hamel: "You cannot control the atoms within a nuclear fusion reaction. We allow people to go in whichever direction they want to go."[80] The fate of Enron is infamous. Its careless, misaligned approach undoubtedly contributed to its catastrophic sinking as if the many flailing oars of unsynchronized oarsmen sank the Enron corporate ship and took many fortunes with it.

So, to replace the image of banks of shackled slaves on an ancient oared ship, imagine a crew of a small rowing boat, the kind of rowing team many colleges organize for their students. Much more happily than slaves, and in perfect synchronization, rowing crews compete as high-performing, disciplined teams. In modern 'crew,' as this form of competition is known, the experienced team operates so well and in such coordinated rhythm that little leadership from each crew's coxswain is needed. The coxswain, the member of the crew that steers the boat and maintains the rhythm, need only exert their leadership to increase or decrease speed, or to call out a member of the crew that is falling out of rhythm or form.

---

80   Gladwell, Malcom. "The Talent Myth." *The New Yorker*. (July 22, 2002).

To describe the cadence needed to sync teams, the military definition of battle rhythm is a good place to start. The U.S. Navy defines and describes battle rhythm as:

> *"A battle rhythm is a process where the commander and staff synchronize the daily operating tempo within the planning, decision, execution, and assessment cycle to allow the commander to make timely decisions. The battle rhythm is the commander's battle rhythm. It is his 'plan of the day.' Furthermore, battle rhythm is a cascading process. The higher headquarters establishes a battle rhythm and, with this, the naval commander and subordinate commanders nest their own battle rhythm. The battle rhythm is not static; as the operational environment fluctuates and variables are introduced into a situation, the battle rhythm may change as well. Regardless, the battle rhythm gives the commander, staff, and organization as a whole a foundation on which to operate."*

Notice the emphasis upon how leadership is involved in battle rhythm. In practice, battle rhythm is a product of leadership. It originates as a clear and purposeful intent from the leader. Like the coxswain in the crew analogy, the leader sets the rhythm. The leader increases or decreases that rhythm to meet the needs arising from whatever the context may be. A company facing a critical external threat, whether a new competitor or a rapid market shift, may have to increase its *execution rhythm* and then slow down again once the crisis has abated. This *execution rhythm* drives the operational rhythm, refreshes situational awareness, and guides the adaptation necessary to remain on the leading edge of change.

To understand the structure and purpose of *execution rhythm* is to grasp a simple conceptualization. Consider a playing field, one in which athlete's both practice and perform as a team. On this field, athletes develop and hone their skills whether in practice with their teammates or in competition with other teams. The field is where the athletes interact. That field may be literal or figurative. For organizations it may be an office building, a factory floor, or a boardroom. It may even be virtual.

Two Japanese management experts, Ikujiro Nonaka and Hirotaka Takeuchi, have recognized the significance of this field of interaction and the need for cyclical assessment in knowledge creation. In their book, *The Knowledge Creating Company*, they point out the need for a rhythmic field of interaction. The authors write:

> "…we need a 'field' in which individuals can interact with each other through face-to-face dialogues. It is here that they share experiences and synchronize their bodily and mental rhythms. The typical field of interaction is a self-organizing team, in which members from various functional departments work together to achieve a common goal."[81]

Self-organization is a healthy and natural characteristic of teams. However, that organization must be nurtured by providing a process where learning and development are synchronized through rhythmic interaction between individuals and teams. This coordinated rhythm serves to accelerate the achievement of common goals. It helps align the organization from top to bottom and across its vertical silos.

ACTIONS:

Identify peak times. What are the peak performance times of the people on your team? What time of the day are they usually most engaged and productive—morning, afternoon, or evening? With the

---

[81] Nonaka, Ikujiro and Hirotaka Takeuchi. *The Knowledge Creating Company: How Japanese Companies Create the Dynamics of Innovation*. (Oxford University Press, 1995). Pg. 85.

exception of important collaboration sessions (next action below) avoid disturbing or distracting them during this precious period. They need to use that time to focus on their tasks and roles. These are the times they are most efficient and get the most done. Don't let the mundane or non-critical tasks interfere with this period of heightened productivity.[82]

Establish rhythm. How often and for what purposes does your team need to meet? When do you all need to get together to plan, brief or communicate information, share ideas, update progress on projects, etc.? Once you know what you need to come together for as a whole team, schedule those things closely together so that it is all accomplished quickly and to a regular cadence. For example, most organizations schedule several meetings on Mondays. Mid-morning is usually a good point of peak period overlap for team members. So, the collaborative work of the week can largely be accomplished within a few hours leaving the remainder of the day and the rest of the week open for focused work that lessens the interruption of individual peak periods.

Close execution gaps. When you establish a project plan, ensure that you also establish regular meetings with the team to update each other on progress, adapt the plan to unforeseen challenges, reallocate resources or reassign roles. Remember the *uh-oh effect*. Most teams don't accomplish much until the mid-point of a project. The Uh-oh effect creates a gap in execution that is challenging to overcome. Establishing a regular rhythm of team interaction meetings focused solely upon closing these gaps well before the midpoint arrives—and regularly throughout the course of the project - is the best way to guide steady progress.

---

[82] Pink, Daniel. *When: The Scientific Secrets of Perfect Timing*. (Riverhead Books, 2018). Pg. 34.

C – COMMUNICATION

"…all we need to do is make sure we keep talking."

– Stephen Hawking (performing in the Pink Floyd song, Keep Talking)

Talking. The way we humans communicate—and how we record the ideas we communicate—has enabled our species to progress from hurling rocks at sabre-tooth tigers to launching spaceships to other worlds. But, hurling words or social media posts at each other isn't necessarily *good* communication. Recent social and neurological research has begun to pull back the curtain on the mysterious world of human communication beyond mere words. Communication is a tremendously complex activity.

So, how do we make it simple enough to put into a few guidelines? Well, the most effective way to improve communication is to provide some organization to it, thus, relating it to the previous section of guidelines. The first guidelines in this section concern alignment. Good leaders consistently communicate the purpose and values of the organization; how the task at hand relates to that purpose and values; and how it all aligns to strategic and long-range organizational goals. Making these simple connections frames the 'big picture'—the first step in the briefing process—one of the four fundamental activities of the Flawless Execution Cycle.

This section is not a guide to speaking or written composition. Those are skills learned and developed over a long time. Instead, this section assumes that leaders already possess such skills in both speech and writing. This section provides guidelines for leaders to employ their communication skills more effectively.

C1 – Establish / Reinforce organizational identity

"You are the Army's leaders, and on your shoulders rests this mission: win our wars. The desire to accomplish that mission despite all adversity is called the warrior ethos and makes the profession of arms different from all other professions."

– The U.S. Army Leadership Field Manual

What is organizational identity? It's a phrase this author likes to use to include several related subjects that often go by the names of *mission*, *purpose* and *values*. Establishing a written organizational identity is universally recognized as a critical component of high-performing organizations. Organizational identity expresses, in a succinct and erudite manner, why the organization exists and what it values most. It's rare to find an organization that hasn't at least attempted to articulate its identity. Some organizations do it well, some poorly.

At one extreme, some organizations only pay lip service to what they might call a mission. It gets reproduced by the HR department and hangs on the break room wall. Most people in the organization can't tell you what it is or explain why it's important. What's more, no leader in the organization models the behaviors and values it expresses. It's a waste of time and ink because everyone recognizes the farce and snickers about it when the 'boss' is out of earshot.

At the other end of the spectrum where the attributes of high-performing organizations can be found, everyone knows what the organizational identity is and leaders communicate it verbally and in writing. More importantly, they model it in their own actions and behaviors every day (*L3*). Organizational identity must be articulated for the whole organization. If you lead at the top of an organization's hierarchy, it is your responsibility to make sure the organizational identity is expressed and communicated well. As management professors Robert E. Quinn and Anjan Thakor have demonstrated, "When a leader communicates the purpose with authenticity and constancy, …employees recognize his or her commitment, begin to believe in the purpose themselves, and reorient." They also point out that, "The change is signaled from the top, and then it unfolds from the bottom."[83] Organizational identity is defined at the top of the organization, but it's not a command and control decision. It begins with the original intent—an origin story, perhaps. That story evolves over time and the history of the organization informs the evolution of its clearly articulated identity.

This guideline's introductory quotation from the *U.S. Army Leadership Field Manual* is worthy of reflection as a statement of organizational identity. It identifies two things. First, it outlines the purpose of the U.S. Army, to 'win our wars.' Those three simple words imply a wealth of meaning—the protection of national values and interests as well as the lives and freedom of its citizens. Second, it introduces a set of values that it calls the *warrior ethos*. Although it does not define or list in detail the elements that make up the warrior ethos, it does identify it as a set of values that supports the mission—to win our wars. Succinctly, that's what organizational identity should do; define the mission and the values.

---

[83] Quinn, Robert E. and Anjan V. Thakor. "Creating a Purpose-Driven Organization." Harvard Business Review. (July-August 2018). Pg. 80.

Leaders must establish both an identity and a set of values—not in isolation, but with their team. If done well, the organizational identity will not only help guide the organization, but recruit others (*L2*) to the cause. Without a clearly articulated identity, organizations run the risk of falling for charismatic leaders whose purpose is their own rather than the organization's. Without an external purpose as a guide for an organization's leaders to serve, the people have nothing left to serve but the leaders and themselves. Good leaders get others to commit to the mission rather than the leader—and then align to a common set values.[84] Leadership should engage the emotions and then rationally pursue a defined course to achieve a mission. As Daniel Goleman, best-selling author of *Emotional Intelligence*, has noted, "…a great leader defines a mission, acts on many levels, and tackles the biggest problems. Great leaders do not settle for systems as they are, but see what they could become, and so work to transform them for the better, to benefit the widest circle."[85] Organizations are not about the leader, but the mission.

Values are also part of the organizational identity. Referring back to the U.S. Army example, the value system is known as the *warrior ethos*. Succinctly, the warrior ethos is the following: "I will always place the mission first, I will never accept defeat, I will never quit, and I will never leave a fallen comrade." It's just four, straightforward principles of behavior that are specifically adapted to the context of the U.S. Army's mission. Most organizations can't simply lift those four principles and incorporate them into their own organization's identity. The context of the battlefield is one that requires a very different set of values and standards of behavior than a beverage distributor or wireless telecommunications firm.

---

[84] Kofman, Fred. *The Meaning Revolution*. (Currency, 2018). Pg. 8.
[85] Goleman, Daniel. *Focus: The Hidden Driver of Excellence*. (Harper, 2013). Pg. 255.

A set of values essentially defines an organization's boundary of behavior. It tells everyone in the organization what they must always do and what they must never do. It isn't a list of platitudes like "we respect diversity." Values that are common or shared within the cultural context of the organization—across organizational boundaries from one firm, non-profit, or governmental organization to another—are not good candidates for a list of values. The best values are those that differentiate one organization from another. Leaders should seek a value system that is a unique to the organization's mission and supports success in that mission.

Can business units, divisions, departments, and teams within a larger organization define their own identity? The short answer is 'yes.' In fact, this author's experience working with teams and other sub-units within larger organizations has demonstrated the value of doing so. Every team or functional group within an organization has its own unique context within the larger organization. Thus, it has a mission—a role to play—that is different from other functions and teams. Defining that mission is essential while articulating a unique set of values may also be beneficial. However, values of sub-units should always align with and augment the over-arching mission and values of the organization. Don't get mired in statements of values. Keep the list short and relevant so that people can remember them.

As a final thought about organizational identity, it's worth reflecting on an emerging theory about firms and the products or services they provide. Harvard professor and best-selling author Clayton M. Christensen challenges organizations to think in terms of what he calls *jobs-to-be-done* theory.[86] The essential idea is to stop focusing on the product or services and its features and shift that focus to the problem a team or firm solves for its customers. It's challenging to develop an organizational identity. It may be more challenging to

---

86 Christensen, Hall, Dillion, and Duncan. *Competing Against Luck: The Story of Innovation and Customer Choice.* (Harper Business, 2016).

articulate the problem an organization or team solves on a perpetual basis. Presently, products and services are transforming. For example, automobile manufacturers are coming to realize that their *job-to-do* is not to make cars, but to solve their customers transportation problem. *Jobs-to-do* is a developing theory, but it provides useful guidance in the volatile and disruptive modern economy. It's worth considering what problem your organization solves for the firm, customer, community, economy, or world and ensure its essential nature is reflected in your organizational identity.

ACTIONS:

Define Purpose. Call it the *organizational imperative*—the reason the organization exists. What function or purpose does it perform? Keep it short. Make it meaningful. Ask your team to be part of formulating it. If it is already formulated, make sure the people on your team or in your organization understand it and, most importantly, believe in it. The purpose allows you, the leader, to lead beyond yourself. Write it on the walls. Refer to it in formal and informal presentations. Explain how what you and your team are doing right now, today, fulfills that purpose. Ask members of your team what the purpose is and what it means to them. As a leader, you must keep the purpose front and center. Do something meaningful—and help your team do something meaningful—that fulfills that purpose every day.

Articulate values. Call these the *organizational principles*. What are the uniquely differentiating values of your organization or team? Ask your team what those principles are or should be and lead them in articulating them. Which of those values are truly essential? Get rid of them if they aren't. A good list of values should include about five things or fewer. Once you have them, model them (*L3*) and hold your team accountable to them.

Check performance. With an organizational imperative and a set of principles, check daily to make sure that you, personally, have acted to fulfill the purpose and acted in accordance with the established values. Take a few moments in your daily routine to identify ways that you might demonstrate purpose fulfillment and values adherence so that you might exemplify them as a leader.

C2 – Connect to the big picture

> *"If any one idea about leadership has inspired organizations for thousands of years, it's the capacity to hold a shared picture of the future we seek to create."*
>
> *– Peter Senge*

Perhaps the greatest challenge of many larger organizations today is the staggeringly difficult task of explaining what the organization is trying to do holistically and how all the many activities within it relate—how the organizational identity, the strategy, and the programs, projects, functions, and daily individual tasks all come together into a singular, purposeful effort. Members of high-performing teams don't ask questions like: What is going on? Why am I supposed to do this? Why does it matter? A preceding guideline (*C1*) addressed why it's important to establish and reinforce the organizational identity. That's the overall purpose of the sum of all activity and effort of the organization. But, connecting the mundane daily tasks and the latest assigned project to that grand purpose is often challenging. Explaining the big picture to your team requires combining several guidelines presented in this book: *C1- Establishing and reinforcing organizational identity*; *L4 - Cultivating situational awareness*; *and O2 - Aligning roles to goals*. The opportunity to explain the big picture formally follows in the next guideline, *C3 - Brief every plan*, which may fit into an *execution rhythm* described in guideline *O6*.

The position of this guideline at the nexus of many others indicates its central importance. Good leaders ensure that their teams clearly understand why their role or efforts matter by aligning the team's daily action to the strategy and long-range vision of the organization and how it all fulfills the organizational identity (*C1*). It's an essential function of 'teaming,' according to Harvard Professor Amy Edmondson, that helps teammates cohere to a shared purpose.[87] By implication, clear alignment assumes that a vision and a strategy have been established.

It's useful to think of organizational planning in three distinct tiers anchored by organizational identity. Because the organizational identity is more-or-less a permanent foundation, it is not part of the three-tiered planning model. Instead, it is the ultimate object of all planning the organization undertakes. Therefore, at the top of the three-tiered planning model is what is commonly called the *vision*. Some organizations consider vision to be a far-off goal that may take decades to achieve. Some mix vision and mission statements so that organizational identity and a picture of the organization's future take on a perpetual flavor. However, leaders should keep statements of vision and mission separate. Instead, organizations should have a more-or-less permanent organizational identity, but a temporary statement of vision that has a horizon of just a few years. Planning to longer-ranges in the modern volatile and disruptive economy is usually a futile exercise.[88] The *Flawless Execution* methodology addresses the processes and structure of how to build an effective vision statement

---

87   Edmondson, Amy. *Teaming: How Organizations Learn, Innovate, and Compete in the Knowledge Economy*. (Jossey-Bass, 2012). Pg. 99.
88   The Flawless Execution methodology addresses the processes and structure of how to build an effective vision statement known as a High-Definition Destination or HDD. But, that is beyond the scope of this leadership book.

known as a *high-definition destination*^{SM} or HDD, but that is beyond the scope of this book.

While the vision tells the organization *where* it is going in about three years (give or take a year or two), the strategy tells everyone *how* it will get there. Strategy defines the few primary objectives that the organization is pursuing at the same time. The *rule of three* is a good one to follow for organizational planning. Your vision should look out about three years while your strategy should address about three big objectives at the same time. However, over the course of the vision's time horizon, an organization can phase in and out new strategic objectives and pivot to market changes and rising opportunities. To communicate the big picture and maintain focus on the most important things, strategy should be simple and easily understood by everyone. Unfortunately, about half of managers in most organizations can't name even one of their organization's primary strategic objectives.[89] Can you name just one in yours? If not, how can you align your team's efforts to those of the whole organization?

Operational, tactical, short-term and day-to-day plans fall into the third tier of planning. So, front line leaders must draw a clear line-of-sight understanding for the daily objectives and tasks to the strategy and then to the vision. But, do it in reverse. Tell them where the organization is going, how it is going to get there, and how today's tasks, or this month's plan supports that strategy. Limiting this line-of-sight connection to just the strategy is a mistake. Companies that stop short of connecting strategy to the vision have demonstrably poorer results than those that do.[90] Large organizations are deep. Connecting the front-line sales rep's daily tasks to the corporate vision may be challenging. So, don't sweat it too much. Instead, make the three-tiered line-of

---

89   Sull, Holmkes, and Sull. "Why Strategy Execution Unravels – and What to Do About It" *Harvard Business Review*. (March, 2015).
90   Pink, Daniel H. *Drive: The Surprising Truth About What Motivates Us.* (Riverhead Books, 2009). Pg. 55

sight connection to the business unit, department, or functional HDD on a frequent basis. Save connecting efforts to the larger organization's HDD for less frequent occasions. But, don't ignore your responsibility to make that connection at least infrequently.

Painting a vivid picture of the future and the long-range objectives is the first step in driving the intentional daily action necessary to achieving them.[91] Leaders bear the burden of making this connection for members of their team.

ACTIONS:

Connect Purpose, Vision, Strategy, and Tactics. Communicate alignment often. Start with the organizational identity, followed by a vision of the future and the strategy to get there so that your team can clearly understand how today's activities and plans drive long-term results and achieve the organization's purpose.

Envision Success. The science of brain chemistry and the function of neurotransmitters informs leaders how to better engage and nurture creativity. Dopamine plays a significant role because, when our brains release it, we feel good and want more. As authors Friederike Fabritius and Hans Hagemann in their informative book *The Leading Brain* have suggested, "…a vivid image of success can sometimes trick your brain into believing you've already reached your destination before you've even taken the first step. Instead of celebrating prematurely, the brain releases dopamine and increases your motivation in anticipation of impending success."[92] New research has substantiated a practice leaders may use to envision the future with their team. Project your mind into the future and take a metaphorical snap shot of what you see. Describe

---

91   Bruch, Heike and Sumantra Ghoshal. *A Bias for Action*. (Harvard Business School Press, 2004). Pg. 45.
92   Fabritius, Friederike and Hans Hagemann. *The Leading Brain: Powerful Science-Based Strategies for Achieving Peak Performance*. (Tarcher Perigee, 2017) pg. 167.

that future using vivid imagery.⁹³ Ask your team to come along with you in the imaginary journey. Describe what you see in the future and ask team members to do the same. It's a great way to engage a team and help them 'see' the future they will build. Also, invite others to a sneak-preview by making connections to the future in casual conversations with your team.⁹⁴ Those conversations can begin as simply as "Imagine next year that you are sitting in our newly opened facility in Hong Kong…"

C3 – Brief Every Plan

> *"The purpose of the mission briefing can be summarized as the final review of a forthcoming military action to ensure those taking part are certain of their mission, understand the intent of the commander, and grasp his or her concept of the operation."*
>
> *– USMC Definition of a Brief*

Highly collaborative teams are susceptible to a paradoxical fault. The more a team collaborates, the less likely it is to take action. Conversely, centrally controlled or autocratic teams are better positioned to act in a timely manner. However, centrally controlled teams are less likely to act as *effectively* as engaged, empowered, and distributed teams that collectively determine a course of action. In stable environments where competent authority is vested in a central control function, central control works well. Good orders get issued and executed quickly and effectively. However, stable environments are the exception rather than

---

93   Carton, Andrew and Brian J. Lucas. "How Can Leaders Overcome the Blurry Vision Bias? Identifying an Antidote to the Paradox of Vision Communication." *Academy of Management Journal*. (2018.)

94   Coyle, Daniel. *The Culture Code*. (Bantam, 2018). Pg. 77.

the norm. The modern age is one of complexity, ambiguity, disruption and rapid change. In such an environment, distributed action is needed so that individuals and teams can utilize good judgment in a volatile context to achieve common objectives. Unfortunately, collaborative teams empowered to exercise good judgment often get caught in endless idea and information sharing that delays or terminates effective action. Modern experience exposes a deep chasm that separates good ideas from their execution. Leaders must lead their teams from the formation of ideas through to acting on those ideas. In most cases, the root cause of this failure to act is a lack of discipline, the subject of the last section of this book. However, it can also be an unfortunate outcome of highly engaged collaboration.

Being creative or analytical is a time-consuming and often messy process when performed in solitude by an individual. Introduce other persons into the creative process and things get even messier and more time consuming. At some point, decisions must be made and a course of action pursued – sooner rather than later (*K1*). You, the leader, must have a plan. And, you must make that plan clear to everyone on the team. Collaborative teams tend to have trouble achieving clarity. Team members may leave planning sessions with confusion about "what did we actually agree to, and who will do it." As a leader you must *lead* the pivot and establish clarity in the transition from collaboration to execution.

Briefing is a powerful communication tool to help leaders and their teams make this transition. Briefs are highly structured forms of communication and should not be construed as meetings. Briefings are one-way forms of communication that do two important things. First, briefs communicate an objective and the plan or course of action to achieve it. They tell the team what is going to be done; how it's going to be done; and who is going to do it. Second, briefs make a clean break from the work of collaboration—where team members share ideas and build a course of action collectively—to the execution of the course of action. In other words, briefs mark an end to the deliberative mindset and transition into an implemental mindset discussed in guideline O5. Intensive collaboration, especially in complex undertakings, creates ambiguity. If leaders do not establish a clear end to the collaborative planning phase to the structured accountability needed to execute, confusion and friction may arise. Individual team members may not clearly understand what the last decision was, who was responsible to act on it, or even if changes to a course of action are still open to revision. There is a time to collaboratively decide what to do and then another time to do it. Leaders are responsible for making it clear to their team which is which.

The brief dispels confusion by laying out a final course of action. Briefs are not meetings. The time for debate is over. Thus, briefs are short but significant because they align the team toward the objective and provide the clarity necessary for aligned execution. Briefs are an experience, too. It's not enough to simply e-mail a copy of the final plan to the team. Briefs should be live and attended by the whole team. Like the starter gun in a race, the brief signals that it's time to get to work. Of course, every plan is subject to change or adaptation as the context demands. Thus, an established *execution rhythm* (O6) provides the structures and processes to effectively adapt and change a plan *during* its execution.

Briefing is a time-tested communication structure that is too often overlooked. Good briefing practices are needed now more than ever because of the highly complex activities in most organizations. The modern matrixed organization suffers deeply from the lack of good briefing practice. In my and my colleagues' experience, many of the organizations we've worked with have matrixed structures where a single individual may serve as a team member on multiple project teams, all with different, unaligned, and disconnected objectives. Individuals with divided and often task-saturating demands across multiple projects need clarity. They need a brief at the beginning of the execution phase of any project. And, they need a brief when they periodically meet to adapt and review progress, to help them re-orient to the task at hand. It is not uncommon to hear one team member whisper to another at the beginning of a meeting: "Why are we here?" The brief solves that problem.

Briefs should help teams visualize success repeatedly throughout the course of the execution of a plan. "The more vividly you can visualize how the scenario you create will play out," writes Ray Dalio, "the more likely it is to happen as you plan."[95] Briefings should help teams walk through the actions they will take collectively so that the actions that must be taken, both individually and collectively, occur smoothly. Briefs help eliminate friction. As research has shown, comparisons between successful and unsuccessful teams demonstrate that successful teams perform mental visualizations and, perhaps, even physically walk through the planned actions whereas unsuccessful teams did not.[96]

Briefs should be short - only about 15 minutes. At a minimum, a brief should cover the following three essentials: 1) clearly communicate the objective and how it aligns with the organization's mission, vision, and strategy; 2) clearly state the objective to be accomplished by the team; and 3) review the course of action (*O4*) highlighting *who*, will do *what*, and by *when*. The *Flawless Execution* Cycle (*Appendix A*) highlights a five-step briefing process in greater detail.

ACTIONS:

Communicate the vision. Whether briefing a small project or a grand organizational vision, leaders must help the members of the organization visualize what needs to be done and what success looks like. There

---

95 Dalio, Ray. *Principles*. (Simon & Schuster, 2017). Pg. 500.
96 Coyle, Daniel. *The Culture Code: The Secrets of Highly Successful Groups*. (Bantam, 2018). Pg. 196.

are many communication techniques that can help perform this function—speeches, videos, posters, books, plays, and so forth. However, briefs are a simple and effective method that provide an opportunity to communicate the vision of the organization to the team. Briefs are especially helpful in connecting long-range organizational visions to daily activities. One of the critical activities of good leaders is to communicate the vision simply and frequently. The brief is a perfect format for doing so. It provides the structure to include the grand vision as a context for the more mundane and limited projects that must be performed to achieve it.

Use consistent structure. Focus and attention are difficult for people to maintain, especially in chaotic, demanding, and task-saturated environments. Briefs should always be delivered in a familiar structure so that listeners can attend to the information and organize their notes and thoughts more easily. When people know the format of the information, they can attend to it quickly and efficiently. Refer to the three essentials noted above and ensure you present each in a familiar sequence and format when briefing your team.

C4 – Establish a Communication Plan

> *"The single biggest problem in communication is the illusion that it has taken place."*
>
> *– George Bernard Shaw*

How many ways can you communicate? It is worth stopping for a moment and thinking carefully about that simple question. Homo sapiens' default method of communication is verbal—the spoken word from one person to another. Thousands of years ago, we invented writing. That didn't really catch on until the widespread use of the printing press. Such forms of communication seem obvious, but they leave some other important forms of communication out. What about drama or plays? Speeches? Print media comes in a vast array from newspapers to books, to pamphlets, wallet-sized tri-folds, posters, billboards, and more.

But that's all 'old school' now. How many different forms of communication do you use in your typical workday? There's email, texting, telephone (hardline, cell, VOIP etc.), and a myriad forms of video conferencing. Of course, there's a host of social media platforms, too. You can take a picture of a sketch you drew on a cocktail napkin and transmit that to anyone, anywhere, instantaneously. You could even open a video conference and doodle or present slides or photos on a shared, collaboration screen so that everyone could 'see' your idea in real time anywhere around the globe or even in orbit around the earth. With all that technology, communication isn't a problem…or is it?

The problem with communication is that it's too easy. Anyone can create content instantly and share it ubiquitously through myriad media. There is a cost in time and in focus to receive and interpret all that information. As a result, we become overwhelmed. Our limited focus and mental bandwidth cannot handle it all. Many individuals and teams muddle through in a world of communication overload. I often ask clients how many emails they receive in a day and how many unread emails they have sitting in their inbox. It is not unusual for both answers to be in the hundreds. Once, I listened as a project manager lamented her inability to read all her emails. I asked how she communicated with her team if her inbox was overwhelmed. She said, "We use text messages." That exchange helped me realize how useful a *communication plan* can be.

What is a communication plan? It should be much more than a plan to broadcast information or marketing content. Instead, it should be a plan that lays out how a team will utilize various channels or media to communicate and exchange information among its members. In other words, instead of using a random form of communication without knowing the probability of a message reaching a receiver or, worse, broadcasting a message through every conceivable communication channel, a communication plan helps teams communicate efficiently, effectively, and intentionally. There are two fundamental assumptions that communication plans take into consideration—that not all information is equal in importance and that not all channels or media are equally effective. An important, but lesser consideration is to realize that different organizations use communication channels differently and for different purposes. Texting may be a great means of communication for one team, but inadequate for another. Consequently, this guideline can only offer general guidance rather than prescribing specific channels for specific purposes.

The intent of a communication plan is to help you focus on the most effective channels of communication, prioritize them, and articulate how they are best used so that leaders and teams can reduce the time they spend communicating and increase the time they have for actually getting things done.

The basic idea of a communication plan can be exemplified by this author's experience on the bridge of a nuclear-powered aircraft carrier. As an officer-of-the-deck on such a ship, this author had the authority of the Captain in navigating and conducting daily operational activities. Running an aircraft carrier is a challenging technical feat, but more so a challenge of coordination. Disciplined and organized communication is essential. An officer-of-the-deck must communicate and coordinate with other ships at sea, aircraft operations among the more than ninety aircraft onboard, and the multitude of departments within the ship going about their often-conflicting daily operational requirements—all while dodging storms, other ships, and shallow water. Around the officer-of-the-deck is a large team fulfilling a variety of roles. Communication among that team is formal and disciplined.

It must be because of the busy, task-saturating nature of the job and the inherent danger of mistakes that might arise from poor communication. The bridge of an aircraft carrier operating at sea is a tense, fast-paced, complex, and unforgiving environment. It is not friendly to situational ambiguity. Consequently, ambiguous communication cannot be tolerated. This is not a context that most organizations will encounter, but military communications management provides some valuable lessons to consider for any organization.

In addition to the people surrounding the officer-of-the-deck are dozens of different high and low-tech methods of one and two-way communication. There are ship-to-ship radio and satellite 'phones' to talk openly with civilian ships nearby and through encoded, secret frequencies to other Navy ships. The radios are usually black and the encoded phones red (you don't want to confuse such things). There are also a variety of handsets here and there to open direct channels to the different functions on the ship. One might be set to the aircraft control tower (essential during flight operations); another to central control where the ships engineering functions are managed; another to the combat information center, where all the tactical information is managed and controlled; one to the Captain's cabin so that he or she can be quickly reached when needed…and many more. There is also a telephone system that works just like that in most any office anywhere. Of course, there are also secure forms of e-mail. And, even in this high-tech age, there are useful and highly reliable low-tech forms of communication including flashing light signals that use Morse code; a 'bag' of flags to fly on the mast to transmit simple messages from ship to ship; and signal flags for semaphore messaging.

Then there are critically important forms of one-way communication. If we are all having a bad day, there is a general quarters alarm that, once sounded, will launch five-thousand sailors to their battle stations all over the ship. That alarm, and others, is part of the 1MC system which is a ship-wide array of speakers set in every compartment so that no one can miss or ignore a broadcast message or alarm. The 1MC is used for a variety of emergency, routine, and special messages including short chats from the captain to the whole crew. On top of all that, there's a closed-circuit video system and a studio for producing live and recorded video programs.

So, if you had access to all that, would you just use e-mail? And, if you did use other forms of communication, how and when would you use them and to what audiences or for what purposes? Those are the questions a communication plan must answer.

Another important component of a communication plan is determining a prescribed lexicon and an appropriate level of communication discipline and brevity. Words mean things—or at least they should. If the language a team or organization uses isn't precise, ambiguity may arise. It is not uncommon for different teams or organizational functions to use the same words and phrases, but have a very different understanding of what those words or phrases mean. If in some businesses one team uses the word 'profit' and another uses 'margin' but one means 'net profit margin' while the other means 'operating profit margin,' there can be an important difference. Sloppy use of language can yield confusion, poor decisions, or even disaster. It all depends upon what's at stake—low stakes can endure sloppy language, high stakes cannot.

Did you ever hear a military veteran pronounce the number 'nine' as 'niner' and think 'What's up with that?' Imagine you are a soldier calling in precise latitude and longitude coordinates over a garbled radio transmission or with a high level of background noise, 'five' can sound like 'nine.' If something that simple gets misheard, then bombs can fall in the wrong place or emergency medical assistance can fail to arrive where it's needed. How high are the stakes for you, in your particular context? If it is high, words matter because the integrity of the information being transmitted is critical. Leaders should consider defining their team or organization's lexicon so that the level of precision meets the need.

The point of this guideline is for you, the leader, to be intentional in planning how your team should best communicate with each other to improve communication quality and diminish its burden and disruptiveness.

ACTIONS:

Define the lexicon. In the early years of this author's military career, I was overwhelmed at the use of acronyms. It is quite possible to construct a complete, complex sentence using only acronyms spiced here and there with a verb or two and some articles and prepositions. Military jargon and acronyms form the building blocks of a unique and perplexing language. Most organizations suffer some degree of highly specialized language as well. Imagine that you are newly hired into your organization or just joining the team you lead. Will you understand what is being said? How helpful would it be to have a document to reference that defined and explained the jargon, terminology, and acronyms of the organization? As a consultant, this author has encountered unique terminology in every client he has ever worked with. In fact, I often stop a client in mid-sentence and ask what is meant by a word, phrase, or acronym. Sometimes, I'll ask two people from the same team or organization and get different answers. Think about that.

Determine channels, use, and priorities. Although it is not critical, you might find it productive to sit down with your team and catalogue all the different communications channels (media) you have available, assess whether or not you will or should use them, and decide how best they might be used. For example, email may be the best channel for communicating routine information, but text messaging or phone calls the better media for high-priority communications. Also consider back-up channels for high-priority communications for instances when a primary channel fails to elicit a timely response. To assist you and your team, consider the following types of channels:

- *1-way, 2-way, and collaborative channels*: A loudspeaker is a 1-way form of communication; a cell phone conversation a 2-way; but some software services provide highly collaborative capabilities that include voice, video, text and more. However, do not forget low-tech forms of collaborative communications such as a meeting room with a table or white board.

- *Synchronous or asynchronous*: A live conversation is synchronous whereas an email exchange is asynchronous. A conversation takes place synchronously because it is a rapid exchange. An email exchange is usually asynchronous because a response may be delayed. High-priority, 2-way communications should be synchronous. Low-priority, 2-way conversations can wait and, therefore, asynchronous communication will suffice. Does your communication plan address these differences?

Identify critical communications. Whether or not you need a formal communication plan will depend upon your team or organization's specific needs. However, it is important for all teams and organizations to identify *critical* communications. Critical communications are those that demand immediate attention and, perhaps, immediate action. Like emergency weather alerts received over a smart phone or other media device, critical communication informs others that something important is or might be happening and to look around, take stock of what's happening, and to respond appropriately. In military aviation, the phrase 'knock it off' does precisely this. It alerts a pilot to a dangerous situation and cues a response to act. Critical communications may also be a deliberate act such as the pulling of an *andon cord* in lean manufacturing where workers that identify a potential defect or process error can stop the entire production line to address it. What events or circumstances require your team to respond immediately and effectively to avoid dangerous, disastrous, or otherwise critically impactful phenomena. What is the unambiguous cue to initiate that response?

Organize for brevity. Journalists are taught an important maxim—'don't bury the lead.' The U.S. military uses a communication rule called 'BLUF' which is, like so many things in that culture, an acronym that stands for 'bottom line up front' to remind team members to get to the point. The first line of a story; the first line of an email; the opening of a meeting should state clearly the point. What, essentially, needs to be communicated or discussed? Don't 'beat around the bush'—get it out front. Having a well-developed lexicon can help leaders and teams be direct. The details may follow later, if they are needed.

Engineer chit-chat. It may seem contrary to the efficient management of communication within a team, but unstructured social interaction and chit-chat among team members can be one of the best catalysts to innovative ideas and trust development. Don't over-engineer communication on your team. Instead, engineer an environment that encourages informal interaction. E-mail may be an efficient way to transmit information, but it is a terrible way to share ideas, collaborate, and innovate. For example, small round tables in a lunchroom encourage isolation. Introduce one or a few long tables instead. Give people an opportunity to sit, share a meal, and talk.

C5 – Listen Actively

> *"Listening well has been found to distinguish the best managers, teachers and leaders…Not only do they take the time to listen and attune to the other person's feelings; they also ask questions to better*

> *understand the person's background situation—not just the immediate problem or diagnosis at hand."*
>
> – Daniel Goleman

It is often believed that great leaders should be great orators; that leadership requires emotionally charged, high-energy speeches to inspire teams to greatness. However, leadership success is only punctuated by great oratory. Great leaders succeed not by what they say so much as by what they do. And, leading effective action must be guided by an understanding of complex issues that can only be gained through listening. "Words are noise,"[97] says team performance expert Daniel Coyle. For high-performing teams, leaders must isolate the signal in all that noise. To do that, they must learn to listen. And, it's hard to listen when your own mouth is running. As a leader, what you feel you need to say can get in the way of what you need to hear.

As a young naval officer of 23 years, I was confronted with the challenge of technically out-ranking and 'leading' a seasoned senior enlisted leader, a Master Chief Petty Officer, who had served in the Navy longer than I had been alive on the earth. It is a humbling experience to have a scope of authority and responsibility without the knowledge, wisdom, or experience to match it. Thus, I learned very quickly that when the Master Chief began a sentence with "Now, sir, I'm not telling you what to do, but,…" that I should shut my mouth and open my ears to hear fully and completely what he had to say. Leaders must learn to manage their impulses. One of the most difficult is learning to bite one's tongue—to shut up and listen rather than attempt to prove to others the depth of one's ignorance and foolishness. Leaders are rarely as wise as they believe themselves to be. And, many business schools have taught management students to *talk smart* rather than listen well.

---

[97] Coyle, Daniel. The Culture Code (Bantam, 2018). Pg. 15.

Management scholars Jeffrey Pfeffer and Robert Sutton discovered a curious phenomenon in their research that they call the *smart-talk trap*. They define the phenomenon as when "people engage in smart talk to spout criticisms and complexities..." which, they continue, "...has an uncanny way of stopping action in its tracks."[98] Too much ineffective talk interferes with productive communication. Talk is often an exercise in pontification rather than a serious process of understanding. Smart talk is the worst. It not only wastes time through pontification, it paralyzes organizations by suggesting complex solutions to complex challenges which stymies execution. Although Pfeffer and Sutton's research is almost twenty years old, smart talk is still at work in many firms. The reason that smart talk is so prevalent arises from how business schools have encouraged students to do just that—talk smart. In the past, classroom commentary has been a large part of a student's grade. In other programs and professional communities, such as medicine and the military, the prevailing pedagogy follows a "see one, do one, teach one" process. Pfeffer and Sutton quip that business schools have encouraged a "hear one, talk about one, talk about one some more" process, instead.[99] The result is expertise in talking, rather than in effective listening. As Dalton Kehoe, Communications Professor at Toronto's York University, entreats leaders: "Don't overwhelm them with your rightness."[100]

Listening with an intent to understand lies at the foundation of good communication. Yet, it is not easy to do. Our minds are restless. We sometimes pretend to listen to what someone is saying, taking in only a fragment of what is being said; usually thinking about how to interrupt someone so that we can put forth our own thoughts and demonstrate our own expertise and wisdom, or tell a story that is

---

98 Pfeffer, Jeffrey and Robert I. Sutton. "The Smart-Talk Trap." *Harvard Business Review* (May-June 1999).
99 Pfeffer, Jeffrey and Robert I. Sutton. "The Smart-Talk Trap." *Harvard Business Review* (May-June 1999).
100 Kehoe, Dalton. *Effective Communication Skills*. (The Great Courses, 2011). Lecture 16.

better, funnier or more poignant than another's. As leaders we must suppress this innate tendency to drown someone out with our own thoughts and words. "Listening well," writes Daniel Goleman, the best-selling guru of emotional intelligence, "has been found to distinguish the best managers, teachers and leaders." Goleman further suggests that leaders should "…ask questions to better understand the person's background situation—not just the immediate problem or diagnosis at hand."[101] The practice of focusing on what another is saying is called *active listening*.

Listening actively to another requires focus. Many have argued incorrectly that it also requires empathy. However, there is a growing body of research and rational argument that empathy is not a skill for leaders to develop. As one thought leader, Paul Bloom, has charged, "The problems we face as a society and as individuals are rarely due to a lack of empathy. Actually, they are often due to too much of it."[102] If that statement raises an eyebrow, hold on. Chris Fussell, a former U.S. Navy SEAL and co-author of *Team of Teams* with General Stanley McChrystal, underscores Bloom's position, "…our empathy for those close to us is a powerful force for war and atrocity toward others. It is corrosive in personal relationships; it exhausts the spirit and can diminish the force of kindness and love."[103] These statements may seem counter to what you have felt or believed most all your life, but they are not. The issue over empathy stems mostly from misplaced care and a lack of understanding of the word itself. Empathy is best defined as a capacity to share the feelings of another. Neuroscience demonstrates that highly empathetic people can actually feel another's pain. So, making decisions under the duress of empathic suffering can yield terrible results. Often, suffering arises from poor judgment and failed

---

101 Goleman, Daniel. *Social Intelligence: Beyond IQ, Beyond Emotional Intelligence*. (Bantam, 2006). Pg. 88.
102 Bloom, Paul. *Against Empathy: The Case for Rational Compassion*. (Harper Collins, 2016). Pg. 5.
103 Fussell, Chris. *One Mission: How Leaders Build a Team of Teams*. (Portfolio Penguin, 2017). Pg. 9.

reasoning. It impedes rather than supports problem solving. When we feel pain, even empathically, we seek to alleviate that pain regardless of long-term consequences. Such short-sightedness is not the quality of a good leader.

Active listening requires something other than empathy. It requires *compassion*. LinkedIn CEO, Jeff Weiner agrees. He characterizes empathy as "…when you take on the suffering of others and you both lose." On the other hand, "compassion means making difficult decisions for the good of the organization even when it negatively impacts individuals."[104] Empathy is passive. It just happens to you as you witness the suffering of another. Compassion, on the other hand, is active. You must listen to understand and then take action to solve a problem. Empathy is crying during a sad movie. Compassion is conducting CPR to a victim in an automobile accident. Thus, leaders should use compassion to help individuals understand their circumstances and use reason to solve issues rather than responding to shared, empathic suffering. It requires leaders to understand comprehensively a position or issue and seek root causes to solve it rather than responding to alleviate some symptomatic pain.

So, leaders must resist entreaties from others to be more empathetic. Instead, leaders must make a concerted effort to put aside their opinion and judgment to listen carefully and engage their compassion.

ACTIONS:

Listen to one person daily. If you practice management by walking around, then you will encounter more than one person each day that you can take the time for active listening. But, for geographically dispersed teams walking around doesn't help. So, scheduling time

---

104 Hougaard, Rasmus and Jacqueline Carter. *The Mind of the Leader: How to Lead Yourself, Your People, and Your Organization for Extraordinary Results*. (Harvard Business Review Press, 2018). Pg. 16.

with one individual each day to have a meaningful conversation will not only establish you as a caring leader, but also one in touch with what's really going on in your team or organization. However, don't miss an impromptu opportunity to engage with someone who looks like they have something 'going on' or something to say, yet might be apprehensive in talking about it. Approach them with a simple question, "What's on your mind?" Then follow the tips in the next action item below. In the U.S. Navy there's an instructive rule of thumb for leaders: "A complaining sailor is a happy sailor." The implicit warning is that when sailors stop complaining, you have real issues to worry about. They have become silent because they feel they won't be heard or perhaps even fear reproach for their complaints.

Focus on the speaker. Active listening requires two fundamental cognitive activities. First, devote your undivided attention to the speaker. Body language also matters to both of you—the speaker and the listener. Face the speaker, lean in toward them, use head nods and verbal cues like "mmms" and "ahhs," and don't cross your arms. The second thing to do is to provide feedback. If you are listening intently to understand what is being said and communicated to you, then you should be able to interject with phrases like "Now, help me understand what you meant by…" and "So, what I hear you saying is…" You cannot ask those kinds of questions or make such statements if you aren't listening intently and thinking about what is being said. Thus, you cannot be distracted by what's happening outside the window or checking your smartphone for the latest call or text message. Some additional good advice can be found in the *U.S. Army Leadership Field Manual* which tells leaders "…don't allow yourself to become distracted by the fact that you're angry, or that you have a problem with the speaker, or that you have lots of other things you need to be thinking about. If you give in to these temptations, you'll miss most of what's being said."[105]

---

105 Center for Army Leadership. *The U.S. Army Leadership Field Manual.* (McGraw Hill, 2004). Pg. 76.

Vent in private. Leaders are human. They get caught up in emotions. Both Abraham Lincoln and Dwight Eisenhower had a curious habit. Confronted with endless crises and decisions that, if made poorly, could demand an unimaginable cost, they endured many moments of intense anger and frustration when subordinates failed or vexed them. Lesser leaders would have either publicly or privately lashed out with invective. Knowing that angry rants would do nothing but undermine their efforts, Lincoln and Eisenhower would sit down and write a letter to the object of their wrath. However, they never sent or mailed those letters. The experience of expressing their frustration and disappointment on paper allowed them to 'vent' emotionally. The next day, they simply threw the letters away. Today, it is too easy to write an e-mail and hit send or post a rant on social media. So, don't lash out at others. Do not vent your anger publicly. Take it home and write down how you feel and how you think about the object of your frustration and anger. Put it aside and then throw it away the next morning. Just let it go.

K - KNOWLEDGE

I know only that I know nothing.

– *Socrates*

Socrates had a tremendous impact on western philosophy. He is famously attributed to have said that he knew only that he knew nothing. It's a powerful idea to chew on with our intellectual teeth, but it's not practical to fully adopt his position on knowledge - to reject everything we think we know. We must accept some things as fact if we are to achieve anything in the real world. Finding the truth is more important now than ever because knowledge informs action and actions have complex cascading effects upon everything and everyone around us. Instead, be relentless in your pursuit of truth and remain open to revising what you believe is true.

For decades, management scholars have recognized a fundamental shift in the kind of work performed in the modern economy—a transition to knowledge work. Therefore, how we manage knowledge is an important aspect of leadership in the 21st Century.

We also live in a world where data and information are readily available, but do not necessarily equate to knowledge. Furthermore, the knowledge requirements to succeed in a complex world exceed that of any single human being. Teams of individuals with varying knowledge specializations are needed whereas a century ago, a lone genius could solve a perplexing issue.

Consider the three categories of knowledge made famous by former Secretary of Defense, Donald Rumsfeld. There is knowledge that is explicit and readily available to us—*we know what we know*. Then, there is the knowledge that we lack—*we know what we don't know*. Finally, there is the complete lack of awareness of a knowledge gap—*we don't know what we don't know*. There is a further complication, however, the things we falsely believe are true. We might call this class—*we think we know but don't*.

These gaps in what we don't know and think we know are some of the great challenges leaders face in the 21st century. This section, *Knowledge*, and the following section, *Experience*, provide guidance on how to bridge such gaps and make better individual, team, and organizational decisions.

K1 – Take Action

> *"A good plan violently executed today is better than a perfect plan executed next week."*
>
> – General George S. Patton

> *"Be willing to make decisions. That's the most important quality in a good leader. Don't fall victim to what I call the Ready-Aim-Aim-Aim Syndrome. You must be willing to fire."*
>
> - T. Boone Pickens

'Taking action' ought to be an obvious characteristic of good leaders, but it often isn't. Some of the preceding guidelines have hinted at a propensity for delayed action in many organizations. It may be because (*O2*) roles and goals haven't been clearly established; or (*C5*) leaders are stuck in a smart talk trap rather than actively listening and (*L4*) facilitating collaboration to (*O4*) establish a course of action. But, this guideline addresses action from a different perspective. It isn't always a lack of these other items that are at issue. Sometimes, it's a lack of urgency or a failure to see the need for positive, intentional action. Sometimes leaders incorrectly take a wait-and-see stance or get overwhelmed by information and opinions. This guideline is a rule of thumb rather than must-do. Action requires good judgment, first. However, more often than not, acting beats waiting.

This author has a tendency to get stuck in analysis. It's just my temperament, the way I'm 'wired,' a psychological default position. I like to think about things more than I like to participate in things. That is usually not a positive trait for leaders and it is one that I must remain conscious of so that I can always ask myself if a wait-and-see position is what is best for any given circumstance. Analytical skills are great traits for leaders, but they can lead to inaction. This inactivity is often called *analysis paralysis*.

Some leaders falsely believe that data and analysis can generate safe decision-making in complex environments. That's wrong. There is no such thing as certainty in complexity. Every action is a best guess with some potential for failure. What is certain is that things change with time. Time is a limited resource of inestimable value that may be squandered by leaders who stop and wait for data or pause too long to ruminate over options. Time is valuable and history bears this simple principle out. Both in war and in business, concerted effort over a short period is often the key to success. Some military and business strategists have called this phenomenon the *time-value of action*.[106] As one American Civil War Confederate General has been misquoted to have said, "Git thar fustest with the mostest!"

Although it isn't clear who originated a meme that has been showing up in various social media platforms recently, it's worth quoting for its truth and dark humor: "The road of life is paved with flat squirrels that couldn't make a decision." In defense of squirrels, they are not the only animals that will jump back and forth in the middle of a busy road trying to decide which way to run. They fail to realize that any side is better than the busy, dangerous road. This guideline addresses the danger of the indecision found in the metaphorical 'middle of the road.' In most cases, making a decision and acting on it in a timely manner, even if the decision is wrong, is better than postponing a decision. As best-selling business parable author Patrick Lencioni has observed, "…implementation science is more important than decision science."[107] In other words, execution trumps analysis. The business strategy guru, Michael Porter, makes the same point in his oft-quoted statement that, "It is better to have grade B strategy, with grade A execution, than the other way around."

Execution through ambiguity matters both at the front-line of daily operations as well as at the highest levels of strategic decisions. It requires gathering data, information, and insight to inform judgment that, in turn, becomes decision and action. Too often leaders fear implementing the acceptable or good because they expect the perfect. Decision-making researchers warn leaders to consider that "…data is no more than evidence, and it's not always obvious what it is evidence of."[108] There is always uncertainty. But, taking action alleviates

---

[106] Warden, John A., III and Leland A. Russell. *Winning in Fast Time*. (Venturist Publishing, 2002). Pg. 43.
[107] Lencioni, Patrick. The Advantage: Why Organizational Health Trumps Everything Else in Business. (Jossey-Bass, 2012). Pg. 79.
[108] Martin and Golsby-Smith. "Management is Much more Than a Science: The Limits of Data-Driven Decision-Making." *Harvard Business Review*. (Sept-Oct,

uncertainty. Even when a decision is wrong it draws attention to what would have been right, which allows for course correction. If you find yourself on the wrong side of the road you can still cross to the other side. If a poor decision is made, then learning occurs. Mistakes provide information, too.

Of course, rash, uninformed or ill-considered action isn't what good leaders should pursue either. Instead leaders should have a *bias* for action. They should err on the side of taking action rather than on the side of weighing options and waiting for opportunities. Have a bias for action but be intentional and exercise good judgment. There is no substitute for judgment. It isn't simple. You cannot buy it off the shelf. It is born of experience which is addressed in the next section.

The best argument for assuming a bias for action comes from IMD business strategy professor Phil Rosenzweig and his excellent book, *Left Brain, Right Stuff*. Rosenzweig argues that there are two errors—errors of *commission* and errors of *omission*. Respectively, there are things we do but do them wrongly; and there are things we should do but don't. Leaders often err toward omission, rather than commission, and that is wrong. This is because, he argues, leaders underestimate their ability to influence outcomes. Instead, leaders should assume greater influence and control because the upside is better than the downside. Why? Because there are almost always competitors or rival teams and organizations that have a higher tolerance for risk and will make the big play. "Only by taking chances, by pushing the envelope," writes Rosenzweig, "can companies hope to stay ahead of rivals…playing it safe will almost guarantee failure."[109]

Don't delay action without good reason to do so. And, don't rely on chance to make your decisions for you. Flipping a coin isn't an act of agency; it is the abdication of responsibility. Bold action is usually

---

2017). Pg. 131.
109 Rosenzweig, Phil. *Left Brain, Right Stuff: How Leaders Make Winning Decisions*. (Public Affairs, 2014). Pg. 74.

better than an abundance of caution so long as you are aware of the hazards (*D3*).

ACTIONS:

Bias to act. Ask yourself, "Am I standing in the middle of the road?" Having a bias for action means that when you are not sure, you act instead of wait. It means that you seek good rather than perfect information, make a decision, and execute that decision.

Set suspense. Undecided, but not stuck in the middle of the road? Set a time limit, or suspense, on when you and your team must make a decision…and stick to that date.

K2 – Include expertise and diversity

"…collective ability equals individual ability plus diversity."

– Scott Page

Although having a bias for action can be a factor that differentiates high-performing teams from the mediocre, gathering the right information from the right sources and subjecting it to an appropriate level of analysis is fundamental. Just remember that, as outlined in guideline *K1*, analysis can be a trap that robs you and your team of precious time.

Leaders must include expertise and cognitive diversity to achieve good decisions and develop effective courses of action (i.e. plans) in the complex, modern world. MIT professor and best-selling author of the classic *The Fifth Discipline*, Peter Senge, makes it clear why this is so. "Perhaps for the first time in history," he writes, "humankind has the capacity to create far more information than anyone can absorb, to foster far greater interdependency than anyone can manage, and to accelerate change far faster than anyone's ability to keep pace."[110] It is clear that no complex organization of significant scope and scale can be commanded or controlled by a lone intellect. Steve Jobs understood that, too. "Great things in business," said Jobs, "are never done by one person, they're done by a team of people."[111] A leader's team exists because they are thinking beings necessary for solving complex problems. To ignore the unique perspectives and the raw processing power of their collective minds is an unfortunate mistake. Modern leaders must get, not only their direct reports, but also the extended members of the organization, in the decision-making and planning process. Making final decisions may be the responsibility of leaders, but it is also their responsibility to hear—to actively listen (*C5*)—to a variety of opinions and perspectives to inform that decision-making process.

Unlike the design of teams that was addressed in guideline *L2 - Get the right people on your team*, this guideline addresses the importance of incorporating a wide variety of input to decision-making and planning. It's about making good decisions. Leaders must include inputs and opinions from a diverse spectrum. Challenging and testing ideas is essential while consensus of similar opinions and positions may endanger expected outcomes. Leaders should avoid surrounding themselves and assembling teams of like-minded people. Human nature, however, runs counter to this advice. We naturally seek to associate with and select people like us. Leaders must resist this tendency and, instead, seek the talents, perspectives, and cognitively diverse abilities of a well-rounded team.

In most instances, heterogeneity is superior to homogeneity. To demonstrate this point, a team of researchers took multiple groups of three individuals. All the groups were asked to solve a problem

---

110 Senge, Peter M. *The Fifth Discipline: The Art and Practice of the Learning Organization.* (Currency, 2006). Pg. 69.
111 Jobs, Steve. *60 Minutes* Interview, 2008.

together. Each team of three either had one member that was similar or dissimilar to the other two teammates. The results were clear, the teams with a dissimilar or diverse (heterogeneous) member outperformed the groups composed of similar (homogeneous) members.[112]

As a general rule, where creativity and innovative problem solving is required, diversity is beneficial. We are all unique human beings with different backgrounds, training, education, and experiences. Humans are information-processing and decision-making machines. Because no two life experiences are the same, no two minds see the world the same or solve problems the same way. When we work together in teams, our combined cognitive abilities yield a power greater than the sum of the individual minds. As one of the leading scholars on the power of diversity, Scott Page, has put it, "…collective ability equals individual ability plus diversity."[113] For Page, diversity isn't just a difficult-to-measure, feel-good quality of teams; it is quantitatively demonstrable. "What we create is a function of the information we consume," writes psychologist Ron Friedman. The implication of this, he suggests, is that we consume information and experience. Thus, cognitive diversity arises from the various and continued consumption of new learning and experiences. Friedman also points out that leaders and their teams should continue to expose themselves to diverse mental stimulation to support and continually develop creative problem-solving abilities.

Unfortunately, the modern experience has led many to think of diversity in limited terms—that of race, sex, and culture. That's an unfortunate limitation on the much broader concept of diversity. Although such aspects of diversity provide essential cognitive differentiation based upon life experiences, they leave out many more obvious

---

112 Phillips, Liljenquist, and Neale. "Is the Pain Worth the Gain?: The Advantages and Liabilities of Agreeing with Socially Distinct Newcomers." *Personality and Social Psychology Bulletin* 35, No. 3, 2009. Pgs. 336-350.
113 Page, Scott E. *The Difference: How the Power of Diversity Creates Better Groups, Firms, Schools, and Societies*. (Princeton University Press, 2007). Pg. xiv.

ones. Consider that diversity also includes: personality and temperament, formal education, professional experience, age, socio-economic background, language, etc. Each of these few aspects can be further broken into much broader and richer diversity as well. Formal education provides a good example of a common mistake that corporate recruiters make. Selecting one or just a few academic credentials from a few specific schools may target some high-caliber talent, but regardless of the quality of the school, the educational experience will be highly homogeneous—perhaps creating a large group of candidates trained by the same handful of professors. Such high selectivity creates more homogeneity than heterogeneity. It's worth considering how small your recruiting talent pool is. You may be inadvertently diminishing the power of diversity on your team.

A further point about cognitive diversity regards more than just difference in thought, but difference of opinion—even contrarianism. Teams can be strengthened by frank and transparent dissent so long as team members do not actively seek to undermine a team's efforts. Teams benefit from having at least one vocal 'wise guy,' as MIT professor Alex Pentland suggests, to test assumptions.[114] Such contrarianism can be formalized into decision-making and planning improvement processes such as *red teaming* that will be discussed in guideline *E1*.

So, when is cognitive diversity not needed? Usually in instances where narrow, credentialed expertise is fitting such as in highly technical yet clearly understood cases. Even diversity champion Scott Page concedes that for challenges that are not new, novel, or complex, diversity may not be useful. Instead, you need experts that have proven the effectiveness of their approach and methods. Furthermore, teams of such individuals should share trust and a common language.[115] Page

---

114 Pentland, Alex. Social Physics: How social Networks Can Make Us Smarter. (Penguin Press, 2014). Pg. 40.
115 Page, Scott E. *The Difference: How the Power of Diversity Creates Better Groups, Firms, Schools, and Societies*. (Princeton University Press, 2007). Pg. 10.

clarifies the overwhelming point for leaders to consider, "…if we are not sure of what we're doing, we should err toward greater diversity."[116]

ACTIONS:

Diversity of experience. Although most of the content of this book is based in research and time-tested wisdom, it would have been impossible to compile and write without this author having the experience of leading others. Experience sharpens our focus and understanding of what, otherwise, is just information. It enables us to find the signal in the noise and organize data into actionable information. So, the level of experience a team member has that is relevant to the task at hand matters. However, it is also wise to include rookies on a team because, as Liz Wiseman in her book *Rookie Smarts* points out, those with little expertise are more likely to spot fundamental errors made by those with more experience. Experience tends to narrow focus and establish rigid assumptions in veterans of a given field. Those who are approaching a subject for the first time, however, are not encumbered by such assumptions. Therefore, they may aid in exposing assumptions that are wrong or that have been rendered no longer relevant in ever-changing and evolving contexts.

Diversity of background. Although it is easy and it feels 'safe,' leaders should be cautious to not recruit team members solely from a specific background—especially one like their own. For example, the firm that I have worked in for over a decade is of military origin, and in the past predominately employed fighter pilots. This is a rational approach because the brand that the firm represents is steeped in the fighter pilot experience and its value to its clients is derived predominately from such a background. However, many different military backgrounds are now included as well as those with no military background. Those were lessons learned in the early years of the firm – and learned the

---

[116] Ibid. pg. 194.

hard way. Too much homogeneity diminishes diversity and may cripple an organization.

Diversity of personality. There are myriad personality and temperament assessments available to leaders. It would be impossible to summarize them effectively here or to provide a useful survey of how to utilize and manage personality in an organization. Most of them can be reduced to four primary personality types; of which few people are predominately one type or another. Most people behave according to a rich mixture of these primary types. However, one has been overlooked until recently that is worthy of special attention—the personality spectrum between introvert and extrovert. Surprisingly, introverts in some circumstances make excellent leaders. The management and leadership guru Jim Collins has pointed out the introvert-like qualities of *level five leaders* in his book *Good To Great*. Susan Cain has exposed the mental world of introverts as well and touted their value in her best-selling book, *Quiet*. Cain underscores a useful phenomenon for leaders to consider. She cites research showing that extroverted leaders tend to get better results from passive, introverted teams, while the reverse is also true. The lesson is that for a team of competitive extroverts, putting an experienced introverted leader in charge could be the best decision.[117]

Get front-line input. The former Chairman of the Joint Chiefs of Staff General Martin Dempsey and best-selling author Ori Brafman have introduced a new term that is relevant to all leaders: the *digital echo*. This phenomenon is caused by fast-as-light communications in a hyper-connected, networked world. Before anyone can make sense of information, it begs for a response—a knee-jerk reaction rather than deliberative thought and investigation before a response. Stories without facts to back them up get amplified and fake news spreads. As a leadership principle, Dempsey and Brafman propose how important

---

[117] Cain, Susan. *Quiet: The Power of Introverts in a World That Can't Stop Talking.* (Broadway Books, 2012). Pg. 11.

it is to get a front-line perspective—one they call *radical inclusion*. Radical inclusion is about listening to the people that are there, on the ground, where events are happening right now and bringing them into the discussion so that the truth emerges quickly to negate the distorting effects of the digital echo. Leaders have recognized the value of front-line information and opinion for eons. But our fast-as-light world makes such input more important than ever. Getting people to become part of the narrative rather than excluding them from it is the lesson. The basic ideas are three-fold for leaders—listen, amplify, and include. Succinctly, Dempsey and Brafman instruct leaders to *listen actively* (C5) for the anomalies that are often identified at the front line. Then, leaders must *amplify* what is learned from those anomalies so that others can be *included* in the search for solutions.

K3 – Learn every day

> *"The most effective leaders are those who realize it's what you learn after you know it all that counts most."*
>
> – John Wooden

"Be technically and tactically proficient" is one of the U.S. Marine Corp's leadership principles. It's just one of eleven, but it was the one that stuck with this author many decades ago when I was learning to become a military officer. It stuck with me because I realized that I had little knowledge of the high-tech ships I would soon be serving on. As a student of history and political science in a small liberal arts college, I was going to be an engineering officer in the U.S. Navy. It was clear to me that I was technically inadequate for that role, but I was also tactically ignorant. For a naval officer, being tactically proficient meant understanding how to employ a ship to achieve its mission. Without many resources beyond books to learn such a skill, I started playing table-top naval wargames to simulate combat tactics while reading about modern navy weapons systems. Of course, the U.S. Navy sent me to school to learn more and put me on a ship for years of on-the-job training, but when you think about it I had to master three professional skillsets in my early twenties—leadership and management, naval engineering, and modern naval combat tactics and ship handling. At that scale, it seemed like an overwhelming task. But, as with any major undertaking, breaking it down into daily activities and building the discipline to execute those small tasks every day is the key to extraordinary achievement.

Professionals, especially professional leaders, never stop learning. Life-long learning can mean earning a new degree or professional certification, or it may simply be reading an article or watching an instructional video. Whatever it is, life-long learners incorporate learning activities into their daily plans and routines. They also coach, facilitate, and lead learning activities with their teams. Those may be training programs, informal knowledge-sharing activities, or formal debriefs held after every project or plan. In the twenty-first century, leaders must nurture a learning team to maintain its value to its constituents and its standing in the market. Learning is an intentional, active effort. Passive learning—learning by just being there—isn't good enough. You'll learn by being involved in things going on around you, but you'll learn more if you take a deliberate approach.

Deliberate practice is a phrase that's coming into vogue. It's different from just 'practice' because practice only gets you so far. Lately, there's been a lot of attention around a theory that suggests 10,000 hours of practice are required to master a skill. Assuming that's true—and the evidence suggests that it's highly variable from person to person—then there's an important caveat that is usually left out.[118] Mastery requires that the learner continually seek to identify gaps in

---

118 Nowack, Kenneth M. "The Limits of Deliberate Practice." *Talent Management Magazine*. (November 2015). Pg. 25.

proficiency and work diligently to close them. After a practice session, learners should evaluate their performance, identify what they could have done better and how, and then incorporate that learning into the next practice. That is being 'deliberate' about practice. It makes the 10,000 hours invested more productive. Consider the game of golf. If I, never having played golf, grab a bag of clubs and go out to 'play' golf for years (for a total of 10,000 hours), I will become a better golf player. But I won't master the game if I don't put effort into learning after every round. That's why people pay pros to help them become better players. It's also why executives hire coaches to help them become better leaders. It takes a little effort on a daily basis to build a wealth of skill to deposit in the bank of 'you.'

This guideline is both about you and your team. You must learn every day, as must the members of your team. They are unlikely to do so if you don't lead them through learning opportunities. This guideline concerns learning in general while another guideline, *E2 – Assess to iterate, improve, and accelerate experience*, addresses a specific, formal team learning technique. Some organizations are afraid of investing in the learning of its members. They believe they will expend time and money only to lose them to another organization. Modern organizations need to understand that investing in learning—especially in developing a learning organization holistically—is critical. Loyalty matters, but you must recognize and embrace that everyone is on a journey and that journey is unlikely to end with their current position on your team or in your organization—yourself included. Leaders, teams, and organizations that embrace the responsibility to invest in learning provide something lesser organizations do not. The best talent will choose to join your learning team rather than the others. Teams teach each other, and the better they do that, the stronger and more effective the team.

We humans are knowledge and information creating machines that must continually learn in order to participate in the processes of innovation and improvement. The science and economics of information is a fascinating field that sheds light on why some cultures and organizations prosper and others don't. One physicist at the MIT Media Lab, Cesar Hidalgo, calls the global economy a "knowledge and knowhow amplification engine." That individuals, teams, and organizations participate in this economy, is what propels it forward. Those that do it best, through learning and knowledge creation, reap the benefits. Hidalgo claims (quite rightly, I believe) that "…we accumulate knowledge and knowhow mostly through practice, such as on-the-job experience."[119] His use of the word 'practice' shouldn't be missed because it is less in the classroom and in formal training that we discover or create new knowledge. Instead, it is through *deliberate* practice.

ACTIONS:

Watch, listen, read. Modern media and content platforms are an excellent source of learning, but what are you reading? As a leader, you should always have an answer to that question. Find at least one professional journal or periodical that addresses your professional needs best and read it consistently. You can pick more than one, but don't overwhelm yourself. Read books, too—not just ones that are professionally relevant. Expand your horizons. Read outside your comfort zone. To each his or her own, but a tactic that I personally find effective is to always be reading two books—one in the traditional way for quiet times at home or when traveling on airlines and another to listen to when driving or otherwise engaged in a monotonous activity where reading a physical book is challenging or impossible. But keep the books you listen to lighter and less cognitively demanding. Save the more thoughtful and information-dense books to the printed or e-book kind so that you can pay close attention and make notes,

---

119 Hidalgo, Cesar. *Why Information Grows: The Evolution of Order, from Atoms to Economies.* (Basic Books, 2015). Pg. 68.

underline, 'dog ear,' or highlight passages. All that said, a wise professor once gave me a great piece of advice—"It's better to read a good book twice than two good books." In other words, make reading an intentional and deliberate learning activity.

Coach and be coached. What are you trying to improve upon? Do you have a coach or mentor to help you? Atul Gawande points out the power of having a coach, regardless of who you are or what your qualifications may be. As an accomplished surgeon, Gawande saw that he could be better—that anyone, whatever their level of skill may be, could be better. When he felt that his skills as a surgeon were no longer improving, he employed a coach to come into his operating room and observe him. A coach can provide excellent feedback through observation. "Coaches," he says, "are your external eyes and ears providing a more accurate picture of your reality."[120] That's what great coaches do in sports, but many highly-skilled professions don't employ coaches as a means of learning. Executive coaching has developed into a high-demand profession because of this fundamental realization— that coaches help you get better. Consider finding a coach to help you become a better leader. Furthermore, are you serving as a coach to the members of your team?

Share learning. Establish an informal forum with your team to share new learning. Set aside some time, maybe an hour on a regular basis, but not every day, to exchange learning among your team. It could be to share lessons learned from a recent debrief (*E2*), important points from a seminar or training program that a member of the team recently attended, or perhaps just to share what is learned from a book you or someone on your team read. You could even assign different topics to different team members on a rotating basis so that everyone becomes a teacher. The intent should be to share learning as a team in a social

---

120 Gawande, Atul. "Want to Get Great at Something? Get a Coach." TED 2017. Also in his book *Better: A Surgeon's Notes on Performance*. (Picador, 2008).

forum. It not only develops the team, but also underscores the value of learning to everyone.

K4 – Train and Develop

> *"Unlike factories, trucks, and advertising campaigns, people appreciate in value. Investments in training are strategic bets on your most valuable assets."*
>
> – <u>Talent Wins</u> by Charan, Barton and Carey

There is an unfortunate trap that insecure leaders are apt to fall into. Call it a "self-importance" trap. It is a tendency for leaders to solve their direct reports' problems; to offer their wisdom and pass judgment upon all matters great and small. Like an all-powerful king, you hold court with your subjects who wait in line to seek justice and wisdom from the throne. Like Solomon, you dole out your judgments. That sort of approach to leadership not only makes you important and holds you up above others, it gives you a sense of security—that the team can't be successful without you. Such an approach to leadership might seem satisfying on the surface, but it is a terrible burden that stresses the leader and increases the fragility of the organization. Leaders that train and develop their teams, however, can eliminate much stress and improve the potential for success and mitigate the fragility of teams. Leaders should instead view their success in terms of how well they enable their team to act effectively and solve problems without their direct prescription.

What's the difference between training and development? In short, the former is short term and the latter long. Training addresses immediate needs while development (which includes formal education) is an investment in an individual for the future. Consequently, training has a shorter life span than development. Training nowadays can be considered to have a half-life which some estimates have put in the range of just two-to-five years. That means, what we learn today to do our jobs will be obsolete in about the time it takes to finish a bachelor's degree. Training gets into the specific but temporary details while education is general yet survives and evolves over time. Training also tends to be transactional whereas development is endless. Learning how to use the latest version of a word processing tool is training. Learning to communicate well in writing is a life-long pursuit.

Both training and development of oneself and one's team are shared responsibilities between leaders and the led. Leaders must continually evaluate training needs and gaps in their team and act to address them. Leaders also must intentionally develop themselves and others so their value to the organization is ever increasing. As Paul Zak, Professor of Economics, Psychology and Management at Claremont Graduate University simply states, "Leadership is about developing the human potential around you."[121] He also posits that leaders should ask a question of each direct report: "Am I helping you get to your next job?"[122]

Zak's position isn't new. It represents the stance that the U.S. and many other military forces have taken for generations—but just slightly different. Every leader in the U.S. military, particularly those in the most senior roles, have short tenures—usually on the order of about two years. Thus, military leaders aren't just asking their direct reports if they are helping them get to their next job; they are asking "Am I preparing you to replace me?" For anyone in a leadership position, there is a more personal question to ask: "If I were not in this role tomorrow, who would succeed me?" Truly responsible leaders don't just leave this problem up to other, more senior leaders in the

---

121 Zak, Paul J. *Trust Factor: The Science of Creating High-Performance Companies.* (AMACOM, 2017). Pg. 38.
122 Ibid. pg. 143.

organization to worry about. Good leaders identify and develop their replacements. But, be warned that the leader you report to may have a different opinion. So, share your considerations with the person (or people) you think may be your successor before you invest the time and effort. In many cases it is good to identify several candidates. So, developing your team may best be seen from two perspectives—what are you developing each team member to do in the future and what are you doing to develop those few who might succeed you. In both cases, development is a long-term effort.

What about training? Training is job specific. It's about what you and your team need to learn right now. There is no line that clearly divides training and development. Think of them as a spectrum with training on one end marked "need it now" and development at the other marked "becoming." At one extreme, lack of training may be causing errors and failures. At the other, you and your team are aspiring to become something new, different, or better.

Debriefing (*E2*) is a great tool to help teams identify training needs because, when used properly, debriefs are performed frequently. Thus, debriefs can perform two essential functions in the realm of training—they provide both training and development for those participating in them and they identify gaps in training that need to be filled. Debriefs also help both leaders and led to formulate long-range developmental goals.

Training and development should be inextricably tied to experience. Experience acts as a sort of 'connective tissue' that improves the retention of formal training and education. Just a few years ago, while working with a healthcare organization, I took a few moments to speak with one of the younger administrators who had (as most in the healthcare industry) finished an undergraduate degree to immediately enroll in a graduate program in healthcare administration, investing six years of education before taking his first professional role in the industry.

Reflecting on the course of his career up to that point he realized that he had been taught so much over his 6 years of formal education that he had forgotten most it. But, he said, "I wished I had the experience I'm having now and all that I learned before would have made more sense and I could use all that stuff I've forgotten!" Most of us have probably felt this way at some point in our professional careers or heard others express a similar thought. Formal training and education usually get separated from practical experience—certainly not always, but more often than many will admit. The lesson is that leaders should approach training, development, and experience as complementary. Just sending someone to a school or course without also providing them an opportunity to utilize what they have learned on the job usually results in mediocre returns. Make training and development meaningful and useful to both the individual and the team.

ACTIONS:

Close training gaps. Identify the training needs that are necessary to fulfill roles and accomplish projects and tasks for your team, or individuals on your team, or yourself. If the skills needed are within your capacity to teach, do it yourself (time and effort permitting). If not, you may need to reach into your budget or ask for the funds. Just recognize that time you spend one-on-one with your team builds trust and camaraderie. Conducting training yourself is a great opportunity to mentor your team. Mentoring can be another 'flavor' of training that is closer to the development side of the learning spectrum. A quick approach to this is called *flash mentoring* which requires a learner to 'shadow' a mentor for a day (or just a few hours) to learn from them.[123] Flash mentoring can be done regularly between members of a team providing cross-training that strengthens team capabilities, resilience, and breadth of knowledge. Of course, flash mentoring is a great

---

123 Coyle, Daniel. *The Culture Code*. (Bantam, 2018). Pg. 167.

teambuilding technique too. Training and mentoring are especially important for new members of the team. So be sure to spend more time with them addressing their training and mentoring needs within their first 90 days on your team. Meet with them as their leader at least weekly during that introductory period.[124]

Stop leading…sometimes. "Do what!?" No, I'm not kidding. Sometimes you need to get out of the way and let others lead. One of the great mistakes in organizations is that members aren't given a chance to lead until the mantle of leadership is thrust upon them. How do you expect up-and-coming leaders to gain practice and experience unless you get out of the way from time to time and let them lead? Is there a new project coming up where you could hand the reigns over to someone on your team while you take a step back and mentor them through it? On a smaller scale you could do what one group of leadership scholars have suggested, try a *sit down* technique. Willfully abdicate authority during a meeting or planning session and take a silent position next to a flip chart or white board, marker in hand, ready to take notes on what the team plans or decides on their own.[125] If your team brings you a problem to solve, give it back to them. Tell them to come up with a recommendation or plan on their own to present to you, and then act as a red team (*E1*) for their solution. One of the responsibilities of good leaders is to make themselves 'dispensible'— to empower their team to function without them.[126] The best leaders provide only their intent (*O3*) and then delegate and trust (*L6*) their team to do what is needed and what is right. That's why development is so critical to high-performing teams. The U.S. Army Leadership

---

124 Gostick and Elton. *The Best Team Wins: The New Science of High Performance.* (Simon and Schuster, 2018). Pg. 130.
125 Heifetz, Grashow, and Linsky. *The Practice of Adaptive Leadership: The Tools and Tactics for Changing Your Organization and the World.* (Harvard Business Press, 2009). Pg. 164.
126 Ibid. pg. 168.

Field Manual gets it right: "Train your subordinates to plan, prepare, execute, and assess well enough to operate independently."[127]

---

127 The Center for Army Leadership. *The U.S. Army Leadership Field Manual.* (McGraw Hill, 2004). Pg. 14.

E – EXPERIENCE

*"Life can only be understood backwards;
But it must be lived forwards."*

– Soren Kierkegaard

The *experience* section of guidelines addresses what might seem like an obvious component of high performing teams—experience. To be successful, surely a team needs to include at least a few individuals that have experience doing the same kind of thing or something similar. This is usually true, but sometimes experience may NOT be what you need. Furthermore, even when you need it you may not be able to get it easily.

What is the difference between knowledge and experience? Stumped? Here are some simple definitions—knowledge is *know-what* whereas experience is *know-how*. Knowledge is specific and exact. Knowledge is about how things work all the time. Experience is different. One gains experience by tackling complex challenges. It is a best guess and doesn't always lead to the right course of action.

Here's the problem—how does one know when the know-how is still relevant and applicable? Times change right? What worked yesterday may not work today. Considering that know-how can change over time, can experience be a stumbling block to success? In short, 'yes' it can. As the Danish philosopher Soren Kierkegaard pointed out, we *live* our lives forward. We only *understand* our lives as we look backward. Hindsight is 20/20. Unfortunately, living forward requires us to encounter the unknown. Those with experience may see new things as old things rather than approaching new circumstances with an open, analytical mind.

Military history bears out this negative experience effect. When new conflicts break out, especially after long periods of peace, military leaders employ strategies and tactics that worked in the past. There's an old saw about 'fighting the last war' that usually winds up wasting a lot of blood and treasure because the period between wars changes the context. It is challenging to adapt to new battlefields and weapons because they have not been confronted before and it is hard to predict what each new conflict might bring. The best experience is the kind that takes knowledge of the past and uses it rationally in a new context with a healthy fear that past best practices may no longer be valid. Experience walks a thin line.

Think of experience as a type cognitive diversity. We humans often err when we form teams. We like to work with people like us which is anathema to cognitive diversity. Good leaders make sure a team is composed of a mix of rookies and experts.

As a leader, you cannot have all the right answers yourself. Instead, your responsibility is to make sure the team finds the right answers together and turns them into the right actions. You cannot do that in a vacuum. You must assemble the right mix of knowledge and experience. What follows are some guidelines to help you find the right formula.

E1 – Red Team

> *"The warning that 'you can't grade your own homework' has relevance far beyond the classroom."*
>
> – Micah Zenko

It probably comes as no surprise that the 2013 film *World War Z* is fiction. However, it might be necessary to set the record straight about a scene in that film that might *seem* like it's true. In the film, the character portrayed by actor Brad Pitt encounters an Israeli Mossad agent that tells him about the *principle of the tenth man* to explain how Israel anticipated and prepared for a zombie attack. In an exchange between the characters, the Mossad agent explains, "If nine of us look at the same information and arrive at the exact same conclusion, it's the duty of the tenth man to disagree. No matter how improbable they seem," continues the agent, "the tenth man has to start thinking with the assumption that the other nine were wrong." As attractive and believable as that story might sound, it is just as fictional as the zombies. However, it is an apt description of a behavior that really has been adopted by the U.S., Israeli, and many other nation's military forces—the *red team*.

Red teaming is a simple idea—get someone or a group of people to review a decision or plan and with brutal frankness tell you why it won't work or what its weaknesses are. Red teams play the *devil's advocate*—a centuries-old practice first adopted by the Catholic Church to provide an opposition to candidates for canonization. President John F. Kennedy used similar processes within his cabinet to test courses of action and resolve the Cuban Missile Crisis in 1962. Red teams also test systems, operations, and programs with tactics such as employing hackers to find weaknesses in an IT security system, or sending an agent through airport security to see if they can get through with banned materials or fraudulent identification. Fundamentally, red teaming is about exposing weaknesses and errors *before* a decision, plan, or system is executed or deployed. A similar concept is the *premortem* in which the results of a plan or project are assumed to fail and team members work backward from that failure to identify a cause, then incorporate fixes to the plan.[128]

Why is red teaming so important? We are all aware of the trite yet critical need to think 'out of the box.' Unfortunately, when groups come together to collaborate, they are inherently prone to building a conceptual 'box' regardless of how far outside that box they may begin. As discussion and planning begins, assumptions are made and the options and actions open to the team begin to narrow. In a book by Cass R. Sunstein and Reid Hastie, the authors pull together a significant body of research that points to a startling reality about how group decisions and ideas can be negatively influenced by the first speakers in a group.[129] Those who speak first tend to frame or anchor the subsequent discussions and cascade biases and errors throughout the group's further discussion. Under some circumstances, groups can polarize toward one overly biased or erroneous position and become more biased toward that position than any single individual was before the discussion. Groups might also filter out less commonly held information that is critical to reaching the right decision because groups tend to focus on the knowledge they hold in common and dismiss or ignore critical information held by a few or a single member.

The process of planning inherently drives those that created the plan to fall in love with it—and that may pose a serious threat to success. Utilizing a red team is a technique or process to help mitigate the cognitive biases and errors that groups are prone to. All that's required

---

128 Klein, Gary. "Performing a Project Premortem." *Harvard Business Review*. (September, 2007).
129 Sunstein, Cass R. and Reid Hastie. *Wiser: Getting Beyond Groupthink to Make Groups Smarter*. (Harvard Business Review Press, 2015).

is a handful of people that have at least a general level of knowledge, experience, and expertise in whatever the original planning group intends to accomplish and a few minutes of their time. Red team members should also have no connection or awareness of the collaboration and deliberation that took place to create the plan. This red team, usually no more than 3 or 4 people, is charged with acting like the opposing force. Their task is to defeat the plan, expose its weaknesses, question its assumptions, and point out the gaps. The goal of a red team is to get the original planners or decision-makers to exclaim, "Oh! I didn't consider that," and then take action to address the lapse of reason or mistake in design.

In practice, there are two forms of red teams. The first is intensive and special purpose; one in which an individual or team is tasked to evaluate a critical plan or decision intensely and with significant time, effort, budget and other resources dedicated to the effort. For example, the U.S. Army conducts a fifteen-week red team training school to prepare a small cadre of officers to act as professional red team evaluators. It then assigns those officers as full-time red team resources to major units. Of course, that's an enormous investment in a red team resource—one that is valuable, but not scalable. Thus, a second less intensive form of red teaming can be used to a greater, and perhaps more effective extent in organizations. Keeping a red team to a short, structured presentation to a small group followed by an uninterrupted period for candid feedback and critique can be scaled throughout a team and organization. Although these less-intensive versions of red teaming don't subject plans and decisions to deep analysis, that often isn't necessary. Rather, practicing these simpler and shorter red team sessions for small projects and strategic decisions alike may have a greater and more positive impact on the organization as a whole. Additional guidance for conducting these simpler, routine red teams is part of the *Flawless Execution* methodology (*Appendix A*).

However, there are some excellent resources to learn more about formal, intensive red team practices. Two popular works have been published in recent years. Micah Zenko's *Red Team* (Basic Books, 2015) and Bryce Hoffman's *Red Teaming* (Crown Business/Penguin, 2017) are similar and, to some extent, complementary works. A third is produced by the U.S. Army's *University of Foreign Military and Cultural Studies* (UFMCS) which was originally entitled *The Red Team Handbook,* but is now officially titled *The Applied Critical Thinking Handbook*. Anyone can easily search for it online and download the 250-page document.

The fundamental point of red teaming is simply to seek out someone that isn't biased toward your position to review your work and provide candid feedback. The more formal that process is, the better the quality of the feedback. However, you must always consider the cost in time and effort. You won't likely be able to submit everything for peer or red team review.

ACTIONS:

Quid pro quo. Writing an important e-mail? Drafting a project plan? Then, simply ask a colleague to take a quick look and offer their honest criticism. This is a *quid pro quo* request because you should extend an open invitation to return the favor in the future. Healthy teams and organizations engage in this sort of self-check activity and practice it widely and openly as part of their culture. But, here's a tip: ask only a single person and don't pressure them if they balk or suggest they don't have time. Do not email several individuals asking "Hey, if you have time, would you look this over for me?" Targeting a single individual is more likely to get a positive response rather than broadcasting your request to a larger group.

Conduct a formal red team. Performing the red team can be an uncomfortable process if not properly handled. Adhering to a strict red team process is therefore critical. The basic red team process looks like this:

- Present the details of the plan to the red team.
- Provide an opportunity for the members of the red team to ask clarifying questions.
- Allow the red team to provide criticism of the plan by phrasing their critical comments as an inoffensive question beginning "Have you considered…"
- Accept all the red team's comments by writing them down, but do not argue with the red team or start a debate.
- Once the red team has exhausted its critical comments, thank them for their time and effort; and dismiss them.
- Review all the red team's comments with your team and determine which comments you will address in order to improve your plan.

E2 - Assess to Iterate, Improve and Accelerate Experience

"If anybody shall reprove me, and shall make it apparent unto me, that in any either opinion or action of mine I do err, I will most gladly retract. For it is the truth that I seek after, by which I am sure that never any man was hurt…"

– Marcus Aurelius, Emperor of Rome, 161-180 CE

Complexity is troublesome. It makes things unpredictable. Complexity obscures the future in a dense fog. Often, we must feel our way through, stumbling and tripping here and there, hoping not to fall into a chasm unawares. Complexity can also re-write rules and best practices. What worked yesterday may not work tomorrow. In complexity, learning rapidly and with agility is essential to avoid pitfalls.

Complexity is at an all-time high driving volatile change that is challenging to keep up with. The experience of war has always been that way. One of war's great scholars, Karl von Clausewitz, observed nearly two centuries ago that "Everything in war is simple, but the simplest thing is difficult." It was Clausewitz that introduced the phrase 'fog of war' to the modern lexicon. Even in the early 19th Century, having experienced the chaos of the Napoleonic wars first-hand, complexity was a challenge that Clausewitz intimately understood. He knew that whatever a leader may plan to do, the outcome was uncertain. Or, as "Iron Mike" Tyson has tersely put it, "Everyone has a plan until they get punched in the mouth."

Fast-forward to aerial dog-fighting in the 1960's as faster-than-sound jets enter into one-on-one engagements with each other. Things moved fast. Fighter pilots had to think faster to out-maneuver their opponent. That required a new model of thinking that a U.S. Air force fighter pilot named John Boyd created with his *OODA Loop*. OODA stood for *observe-orient-decide-act* and was intended as a mental model for fighter pilots to defeat an enemy in an aerial battle. OODA enabled pilots to outmaneuver their opponent and resulted in phenomenally better tactical performance and improved aircraft design. Contemporary to Boyd, W. Edwards Demming, the father of modern business process improvement, developed what he called *PDCA* for *plan-do-check-act*. Similar in structure, OODA and PDCA are both iterative models that seek to achieve improvement or an optimized solution.

In the past three decades, iterative processes have developed further. *Adaptive Leadership* is the name given to a problem-solving process developed by Harvard professors Ronald Heifetz and Marty Linsky, and their business colleague Alexander Grashow. In 2009, they proposed a cyclical problem-solving process of three steps—*observe, interpret and intervene*.[130] That same year, MIT professor Donald Sull published his own *Agility Loop* in which he outlined a four-step process of *make sense-make choices-make it happen-make revisions*.[131] Sull attributes his inspiration for the agility loop to John Boyd. Each incorporates an information gathering, decision making, action taking, and assessment cycle. The difference is one of emphasis. They all boil down to a fundamental process of *plan-execute-assess* with the results of the *assess* phase being incorporated directly into the next cycle or iteration. This three-part iterative cycle is both the heart of process improvement and agile adaptation in complex environments. This guideline addresses the central activity of the assess phase. Leaders and their teams must take the time to learn from what they have done or executed. They must analyze what worked and what didn't so they can adapt and improve.

The assess phase has many names. In the U.S. Army, it's called an *after-action review*, or AAR. In business, it may be referred to as a *hot wash* or *post-mortem*. Scholars who have researched the effectiveness of assessment tools have used the term *debrief*. In fact, psychologists Scott Tannenbaum and Christopher Cerasoli conducted a meta-analysis of 46 separate debrief studies to quantify the impact of debriefing as a performance improvement technique. They found that debriefing improved performance by at least 25% and speculated that structured and well-facilitated debriefing may improve performance by as much as 38%.[132]

---

130 Heifetz, Linsky, and Grashow. *The Practice of Adaptive Leadership: Tools and Tactics for Changing Your Organization and the World*. (Harvard Business Press, 2009).
131 Sull, Donald. *The Upside of Turbulence: Seizing Opportunity in an Uncertain World*. (Harper Business, 2009).
132 Tannenbaum, Scott I. and Christopher P. Cerasoli. "Do Team and Individual Debriefs Enhance Performance? A Meta-Analysis." *Human Factors*, Vol. 55, No. 1, February 2013. Pgs. 231-245.

The first premise of effective debriefing is now known as *psychological safety*, an idea championed by Harvard Business School Leadership and Management Professor Amy Edmondson. Edmondson defines psychological safety as "a shared belief held by members of a team that the team is safe for interpersonal risk taking."[133] Team members must feel safe to make honest errors and take innovative risks without fear of reprimand or ostracism. Military aviation discovered the need for psychological safety generations ago because of the high accident and error rates that caused many deaths and the destruction of expensive aircraft. Pilots had to have a psychologically safe debriefing process so that the truth could come out. Pilots had to feel they would not be blamed for their errors so long as everyone could learn and improve. So, psychological safety develops from a culture of non-attribution—one in which people are trusted and systemic root causes for errors are sought rather than individual blame. As one scholar has correctly remarked, "…attack problems by fixing the system, not scapegoating the necessarily fallible human being working in and operating that system, whether or not they deserved it."[134] Leaders that expect a zero-defect environment are, in most cases, undermining improvement efforts because they are destroying the psychological safety their team needs in order to identify the errors they need to eliminate and the successes they need to reproduce. As a classic Harvard Business Review article entitled "*Learning in the Thick of It*" pointed out in 2005: "In a fast-changing environment, the capacity to learn lessons is more valuable than any individual lesson learned."[135]

A second premise of debriefing assumes that you and your team have planned. You can debrief an event as an afterthought, but you cannot analyze the successes and failures of a plan or decision without clear

---

133 Edmondson, Amy. "Psychological Safety and Learning Behavior in Work Teams." Administrative Science Quarterly, Vol. 44. No. 2 (June 1999). Pg. 350.
134 Pfeffer, Jeffrey. *Leadership BS: Fixing workplaces and Careers One Truth at a Time*. (Harper Business, 2015). Pg. 185-186.
135 Darling, Parry, and Moore. "Learning in the Thick of It." *Harvard Business Review*. (July-August, 2005). Pg. 92.

details on what that plan or decision was. That may appear painfully obvious, but many organizations don't have clearly written plans or planning processes to subject to the analysis of an effective debrief. It's a chicken or egg conundrum. Effective debriefing requires a planning structure to subject to the debrief. Otherwise, analysis only produces vague, unactionable results. But a good plan developed according to an effective planning process can't be improved on the next iteration without the lessons learned of a good debrief. The results of a debrief need to feed back into the planning process, thus creating a virtuous cycle of improvement and adaptation.

ACTIONS:

Leaders admit errors. Leaders shouldn't be afraid to admit their errors because they must create a culture of psychological safety. Leaders should be honest about their own mistakes at all times rather than just in the confines of a debrief. Evading accountability for errors undermines the most strenuous efforts to develop psychological safety in a team. Some scholars have demonstrated that leaders that show vulnerability actually demonstrate teamwork rather than dominance over their team and that it is an essential ingredient in developing trust.[136] Debriefs should begin with the leader admitting the errors they believed they may have made and openly inviting their team to help them identify any additional errors. Few actions are more effective in establishing an environment of psychological safety than such candor from a leader.

Debrief to identify and learn from root causes. As noted above, debriefing is a proven technique for improving team performance. But the quality of the debriefing process and its facilitation make a

---

[136] Zak, Paul J. *Trust Factor: The Science of Creating High-Performance Companies.* (AMACOM, 2017). Pg. 156.; and Daniel Coyle. *The Culture Code.* (Bantam, 2018). Pg. 107.

big impact on the quality of the lessons derived from it. Just getting together to talk about what happened and what you might have learned from a plan is good. Structuring it into a root-cause-seeking process is much better. But facilitating that process well is best. In the research cited above, the 20-25% increases in performance are based upon teams following a structured process. The tentative data that suggests improvement rates above 30% are based on a structured process *and* good facilitation skills. As a rudimentary outline, a good debriefing process establishes psychological safety first, then identifies successes and failures. Once a few significant results are identified, teams should analyze those results for root causes and build lessons learned that address those root causes. Debriefing performs two important functions simultaneously. The outputs of the debrief create knowledge in the form of lessons learned that is storable and transmittable to the whole organization. Perhaps more important though, for the team that participates in a debrief, especially when debriefs are part of the team's culture, the cumulative effect is to accelerate the teams experience by virtue of the sharing of ideas in a psychologically safe environment. *Appendix A* provides an outline of the debriefing process used in *Flawless Execution*. For a more detailed treatment of debriefing refer to *The Debrief Imperative* by Murphy and Duke (Premiere, 2011).

D – DISCIPLINE

Between the idea
And the reality
Between the motion
And the act
Falls the Shadow

-T. S. Elliot, The Hollow Men

Discipline is where the rubber meets the road for every leader. Without discipline, becoming more than a part-time, distracted leader will be challenging. Discipline is about focusing on the right things at the right time. It is about doing what you must do if theteam you lead is to get where it is going. Discipline relates to the team's ability to carry out the plan as it was planned, its adherence to an established *execution rhythm*, its ability to adapt to change by utilizing *X-Gap meetings*^{SM}, and its capacity to resist disruptions and distractions. It is first and foremost doing what you and your team are supposed to do and agreed to do—even when you don't feel like it. As the poet T. S. Elliot poignantly describes as a 'shadow' in *The Hollow Men*, the disconnect between what we know should be done and actually doing it, is a failure of discipline. Discipline is what connects thought and purpose to action.

Likewise, one of the most prolific, influential, and best-selling business leadership authors of recent decades, Jim Collins, has made a similar discovery. His extensive research into what separates mediocre from great companies is that the mediocre suffer from chronic inconsistency.[137] In other words, great companies know what makes them great and they don't fail to keep doing the things they know lead to success. Great organizations are disciplined while lesser organizations are not.

Shining a bright light to disperse the shadow between thought and act—being disciplined—is much easier when you develop appropriate habits. The chasm of hesitation can be bridged. With apologies to Nike, discipline's mantra should be 'just do it!'

D1 – Prioritize

> *"Principle 2.10: While you can have virtually anything you want, you can't have everything you want."*
>
> *– Ray Dalio, Principles*

> *"People think focus means saying yes to the thing you've got to focus on. But that's not what it means at all. It means saying no to the hundred other good ideas that there are. You have to pick carefully. I'm actually as proud of the things we haven't done as the things I have done."*
>
> *– Steve Jobs*

---

137 Collins, Jim and Morten T. Hansen. *Great by Choice: Uncertainty, Chaos, and Luck – Why Some Thrive Despite Them All.* (Harper Business, 2011). Pg. 138.

You can't do everything. Try, and you'll fail at the most important things. As business coach and author Michael K. Simpson writes, "... if everything is important, then nothing is important."[138] Priorities matter. As a leader you must decide what the most important things are and focus your energies on those things. Otherwise, you will task saturate yourself and your team and burn out.

In guideline *E2*, we met Carl von Clausewitz and his thoughts on the complexities of war. Among many other insights, he also put forth an idea in military theory called the *center of gravity*. The idea came from the physical sciences, that every object has a center of gravity, a point around which an object will pivot. In military terms, Clausewitz observed that a military force on a battlefield had a center of gravity as well. In battle, the strategic objective was to find the opponent's center of gravity and attack it. The center of gravity could be considered the highest priority much like check-mating an opponent's king in a game of chess. A successful attack at that pivot point would result in the enemy's defeat. The idea is still in use today in military theory. It is also a valid means of thinking about business or any other organizational strategy. Crucially, the center of gravity concept suggests that fighting the whole enemy force in war or attempting to pursue a laundry list of strategic options for an organization is wrong-headed. It wastes effort on unimportant things, things that don't drive real progress to the goal. In battle, fighting the whole force wastes lives and creates unwarranted destruction. In business, chasing too many "important" things wastes money, time, and effort. In business, as in the military, the essence of strategy is focusing on the few most important things. As one business strategy professor has summed it up, "The key job of strategy is to create an intense focus on the few things that matter most."[139] It might suffice to say that prioritization is what strategy *is*.

---

138 Simpson, Michael K. Unlocking Potential: 7 Coaching Skills that Transform Individuals, Teams & Organizations. (Franklin Covey, 2014). Pg. 68.
139 Pietersen, Willie. *Strategic Learning: How to Be Smarter than Your Competition and Turn Key Insights into competitive Advantage.* (Wiley, 2010). Pg. 14.

Bill Campbell, the legendary Silicon Valley coach to tech giants like Steve Jobs and Cheryl Sandberg, used a blank white board during coaching sessions and had tech leaders write their five priorities on it. Working through such prioritization of issues became a primary topic of his coaching sessions.[140] This book provides some additional guidance for prioritization. Leaders should align their teams and organizations through a three-tiered structure of planning so that prioritization is possible. At the top, they set the vision. What should the future look like (*O2*)? Then, leaders establish a strategy that explains to the team or organization how it will get to that future. Finally, leaders delegate and trust (*L6*) members of the team or successive levels in the organization to decide what needs to be done to execute the strategy. These three levels of planning create a clear line-of-sight between what needs to be done today and tomorrow to achieve the vision that may be years into the future. Furthermore, it enables prioritization. Things that don't align to that three-tiered structure may not be as important as once believed. That's the essence of Steve Jobs' famous quote that introduced this guideline. Prioritization is about making smart choices to eliminate those things that are not essential. However, it's all easier said than done. The world provides opportunities and we, like a dog suddenly noticing a squirrel, forget our focus and chase after something that has captured our attention. People, teams, and organizations are easily distracted. We tend to heap on new tasks and responsibilities because they seem important. But, when tested against a three-tiered planning structure, we may be better able to evaluate how relevant those things really are. Furthermore, effective prioritization helps teams manage task saturation. Also consider that this same three-tiered structure is easy to communicate and supports guideline *C2* directly.

---

140 Schmidt, Rosenberg, and Eagle. *Trillion Dollar Coach: The Leadership Playbook of Silicon Valley's Bill Campbell.* (Harper Business, 2019). Pg. 46.

ACTIONS:

Design the future. Leaders must describe the future state they are leading towards. That can be a grand vision for leaders at the top of large organizations several years into the future. For leaders in the middle, it may be a description of the success of the division, department, or function and how it will change over time. For front-line leaders, that future might describe how the team works, its standing when compared to other teams, or what the culture and esprit de corps of the team will develop into. Whatever that future looks like, leaders need to craft that future with enough detail to provide clear intent about what needs to be accomplished. It shouldn't be a single, simple sentence. It should be more like a paragraph or a bulletized list of five or ten things that, when taken together, form a holistic vision of the future. In his classic work *Management* (1954), Peter Drucker provided a good, holistic structure for organizations to consider when designing the future. It has been updated to meet the needs of modern businesses and organizations. Smaller teams can use all or portions of it as well, perhaps scaled down, to consider how to best describe their future. Drucker's modernized key areas are: marketing, innovation, human resources (talent), financial resources, physical resources, productivity, social responsibility, and profit requirements.[141] A holistic vision can be described as a 'designed' future because it provides an essential blueprint that communicates intent in these or similar areas.

Identify a strategy. With a clear vision of the future set, leaders should facilitate (*L5*) the identification of a strategy to achieve it. A strategy is just the few priorities an organization or team believes will be most effective in pursuit of the vision—the designed future. Steve Jobs popularized a notion that originated from one of the most respected business strategy experts, Michael Porter. In a classic article published in the Harvard Business Review in 1996, Porter succinctly and clearly

---

141 Drucker, Peter F. *Management, Revised Edition.* (Collins Business, 2008). Pg. 105.

stated that "The essence of strategy is choosing what *not* to do."[142] However, it's also important to point out that Porter also noted, in reference to guideline *K1*, "It is better to have Grade B strategy with Grade A execution, than the other way around." Why? Because a team or organization that executes and assesses their performance through regular debriefing (*E2*) can adapt or refine a strategy more quickly than one that fails to make progress toward their vision via a first-rate strategy. As a rule of thumb, teams and organizations should identify about three major strategic objectives to execute simultaneously. These few objectives are the priorities to execute on immediately. Eliminate peripheral desires and temptations. Establish a rhythm (*O6*) and debrief to assess progress and validate the strategy. If it isn't getting your team to the vision, then don't be afraid to change the strategy. That's how Grade B strategies evolve into Grade A strategies.

Importance and Urgency. A clever and useful prioritization tool is said to have been developed and used by Dwight Eisenhower. It has come to be known as the *Eisenhower Box* and stems from a quotation attributed to the 34th President of the United States. He once said that, "I have two kinds of problems, the urgent and the important. The urgent are not important, and the important are never urgent." Considering the difference between urgency and importance a simple quadrant can be formed to qualify four separate categories and prescribe action. They are:

1. Important and Urgent: Do it immediately and personally (*K1* – Bias to act).

2. Important, but not urgent: Set a suspense date (*K1* – Set suspense).

3. Unimportant but urgent: Delegate it to someone else (*L5* – Delegate and trust).

4. Unimportant and not urgent: Drop it (*D1* – Task shed)

---

142 Porter, "What Is Strategy?" *Harvard Business Review*. (Nov-Dec 1996).

Task Shed. Have you ever taken an inventory of all the things you and your team do on a regular basis? How many of those things are important? Task shedding asks you to do just that—inventory the things you do, prioritize them, and suspend or stop doing those things as the circumstances demand. A task shedding protocol can be organized into four categories:

- *Must Do*: These are the things you should never fail to do. They are critical to the mission of the team or organization and 'keep the business doors open.'
- *Should Do*: These are almost 'must do's,' but if you failed to do them once or suspended doing them for a short period of time, the world wouldn't end. However, you should only suspend doing them in emergency situations.
- *Good to Do*: These are 'value add' activities. But they aren't critical and can be suspended during periods of high task saturation.
- *Don't Do*: Stop doing them now. They add no value.

02 – Focus

> *"It's not enough to be busy, so are the ants. The question is, what are we busy about?"*
>
> *– Henry David Thoreau*

"The twenty-first century cult of busyness and the attendant drama of urgency—the notion that only crisis carries meaning—has eclipsed in many organizations the value

of moving slowly in order to separate the information from the noise, the essence from the distractions."[143]

– *Elizabeth Samet*

Stop thrashing! "Thrashing" is a computer science term that describes a phenomenon when a system's memory is consumed solely in managing programs such that no meaningful processing work is performed. Computer scientists Brian Christian and Tom Griffiths characterize this sort of management work as *meta-work*. Both human and computer systems are subject to thrashing when the meta-work, the work required to manage work, overwhelms the work itself.[144] Some meta-work is essential and healthy. If you sit down to write a list of things you need to get done every morning—a simple form of planning—you are doing meta-work. You are spending time organizing your day so that you can spend that day wisely and focus on the right activities and order them efficiently. Teams and organizations all must perform meta-work as part of the logistics and coordination of the real work that must get done. Sometimes teams become paralyzed by meta-work; meetings to plan meetings, for example. Those kinds of teams and organizations both look and act busy, but the things that are keeping them busy may not be producing results. High-performing teams manage the necessary and appropriate meta-work efficiently, so they can focus on the real work that needs to get done.

So, there's work, and then there's the meta-work to coordinate and make that work most effective and efficient. In a knowledge economy, efficiency and productivity require careful thought. They require focus. Leaders should understand the difference between shallow, low-effort and deep, high-effort, cognitive work. Shallow cognitive

---

143 Elizabeth Samet (Editor). *Leadership: Essential Writings by Our Greatest Thinkers.* (Norton, 2015). Pg. 107.
144 Christian, Brian and Tom Griffiths. "Algorithms to Live By: The Computer Science of Human Decisions." (Henry Holt, 2016). Pg. 120.

work is easier than deep work—like answering an email, sending a text, signing into a virtual meeting, etc. Unfortunately, it is not uncommon that examples such as the preceding consume much of the time of the average worker. Cal Newport, a computer science professor at Georgetown University, addresses a tragic paradox in his best-seller, *Deep Work*. Newport proposes what he calls the *deep work hypothesis*. "The ability to perform deep work is becoming increasingly rare at exactly the same time it is becoming increasingly valuable in our economy. As a consequence, the few who cultivate this skill, and then make it the core of their working life, will thrive."[145] That's a clarion call to leaders who want to build high-performing teams. Such leaders need to create an environment where deep work is possible rather than crushing it with task-saturating meta-work.

Deep work is focused, effortful, and undistracted. A related idea is *flow*, a psychological theory that people are happiest when they are in a state of concentration or complete absorption with the activity at hand and the situation. It is a state in which people are so involved in an activity that nothing else seems to matter.[146] Flow can produce high-quality, innovative or creative output. Deep work and flow should be nurtured. Yet, most work environments undermine the capacity for individuals to reach such states. As a leader, you can't force someone into a state of flow, but you can set the right environment for it to blossom.

But first, you need to understand when deep work or flow is needed and when it is not. Some work requires management of distraction—it's what the work is all about. For instance, this author used to lead a team whose function in a large Fortune 500 corporation was solely meta-work. Our job was to coordinate thousands of service

---

145 Newport, Cal. Deep Work: Rules for Focused Success in a Distracted World. (Grand Central Publishing, 2016). Pg. 15.
146 Csikszentmihalyi, Mihaly. *Flow: The Psychology of Optimal Experience*. (Harper and Row, 1990).

technicians to repair appliances in people's homes across many states. Some team members performed planning tasks. Such work was deep work where service technicians had to be matched with customer needs, appointment time frames, geographic locations, and myriad other details. But, once the plan was put into action, other team members had to adapt and adjust that carefully constructed plan to changing needs and circumstances. The latter was quick, decisive work prone to constant distraction and minor crises. Leading such a functionally bifurcated team, I had to create two very different environments for each to perform at their best. The planning function needed undistracted focus while the team that managed the workforce in real time had to expect disruption and even anticipate it. Both my business and military experience underscore that planning and execution are important, but different activities. Planning should be intentionally focused and proactive whereas, execution is often reactive and distracted. Leaders must recognize the differing needs and context of each phase and engineer the best environment for both.

Unfortunately, in our hyper-connected world, like the teams I used to lead, connection is commensurate with distraction. Connection is essential, and so is deep work, flow, and reflection. The challenge for leaders is balancing it all. Roles that are oriented more towards deep work, require disconnected time for focus, concentration, and, hopefully, a state of flow. Roles that coordinate, respond to crisis and other emergent phenomena, need to be connected and, therefore, distracted, to perform their function. In some contexts, the role of senior leaders is to interpret data and opinion, perhaps dozens or hundreds of times a day, and make decisions that others will execute. As a senior military officer, I often found what I called 'holding court' one of my principle roles because military cultures tend to formally manifest decision-making power at the top of the organization. I would sit behind my desk while my direct reports and other members of my unit would file in with one issue after another seeking my 'adjudication.' It was formal and set up with appropriate representatives and data so that I could make a deliberate, but quick decision. Judges in court rooms perform the same kinds of decision-making roles. Thus, court rooms are highly structured both physically and administratively to support that single decision maker at the center of a network of inputs and communication channels. As a leader, you must evaluate the competing needs for deep and shallow work in order to establish an environment conducive to each, whatever the extreme.

Multi-tasking is a symptom of distracted work. It is not heroic. Multi-tasking is anathema to deep work. So, don't encourage it on your team. Most neuroscience and psychological studies conclude that multi-tasking is probably impossible for humans to perform. We only fool ourselves into thinking we can multi-task on cognitively demanding activities. Instead, what we are really doing is switching back and forth rapidly between tasks which is proven to incur a cost in time and quality. In one study, managers that believed in their abilities to multi-task actually performed worse than those that did not.[147] Another group of researchers found that 65% of the managers they studied failed to complete their most important tasks.[148] For individuals, the lesson is to prioritize (*D1*) and tackle one thing at a time. Because teams and organizations, unlike individual humans, can multi-task to some degree, they can tackle a few big strategic things, usually about three, at one time.

Furthermore, be careful of leading a team that wears task saturation as a badge of honor. Being so busy that you are overwhelmed is not productive. Busyness can be a sign of things other than productive work. It may be a sign of being so overwhelmed with tasks that teams and individuals are expending what energy they have on things that are

---

147 Ophir, Nass, and Wagner. Proceeding of the National Academy of Sciences of the U.S. 2009.
148 Hougaard, Rasmus and Jacqueline Carter. *The Mind of the Leader: How to Lead Yourself, Your People, and Your Organization for Extraordinary Results*. (Harvard Business Review Press, 2018). Pg. 46.

not the most important. That may be because the team doesn't know what the priorities are or that they are selecting easier, less important tasks rather than the more difficult, essential ones. It may also be an expression of nervous energy. In some circumstances people do things to keep their minds off other worries. Doing something, even when it isn't productive, feels better than doing nothing when you aren't sure how to address an urgent, challenging issue. It's usually better to stop and take time to plan or strategize about how to tackle a challenge than jump headlong into misaligned or counterproductive activity. There may also be hazards to ill-considered activity which can be mitigated through guideline *D3 - Risk smart*.

Stop, breath, prioritize, focus, then do.

ACTIONS:

Schedule wisely. Scheduling your team's time is like loading a moving truck. If you think through how things are going to fit, then you can get a lot more in the limited space than if you just throw things in haphazardly. Scheduling work is the same. Group the small things together to make room for the larger items. There is an idea in computer science called *interrupt coalescing* which simply means that you don't do simple, unimportant and non-urgent tasks immediately. Instead you save them all up and tackle them all at once at an appropriate time. It is like saving all the bills you receive over the course of the week until Saturday morning when you have a few moments to sit down and pay them all at once.[149] That's a much more efficient way to handle such tasks that minimizes the time and focus costs of switching from one task to another each time you receive a bill. It is the same for regular meetings and other shallow or meta-work that you and your team perform on a regular basis. For instance, hold all the weekly meetings

---

149 Christian, Brian and Tom Griffiths. Algorithms to Live By: The Computer Science of Human Decisions. (Henry Holt, 2016). Pg. 126.

back-to-back on the same day to free up the rest of the week for deeper work with fewer interruptions. This also frees individuals on your team to make their own decisions about when to tackle deep work. You might also declare an *interruption hiatus*—a time of the day where teammates will refrain from interrupting their colleagues, except for important matters, so there is more time for deep work.

Set expectations of availability. Leaders need time to reflect and focus, too. Open-door policies are great ideas, but often impractical. You need to let your team know when you are available and what sort of responsiveness to expect.[150] Perhaps your open-door policy is just that—when your door is open, anyone is welcome to interrupt you, but when it's closed you need focus time. So, they should only interrupt for important and urgent issues. The same goes for phone and other virtual forms of communication. Should you set an example for your team and stop answering emails at a certain time of the day or evening? What about texts and phone calls? This is a reciprocal issue between you and your team as well. When should they expect to be free from being interrupted by you and your non-urgent communications?

D3 – Risk Smart

> *"...The only mistakes you can learn from are the ones you survive."*[151]
>
> – Jim Collins and Morten T. Hansen, Great by Choice

Risks are inherent in everything we do. You can't get out of bed in the morning without some small amount of risk. But the word 'risk' is often

---

150 Kethledge, Raymond M. and Michael S. Erwin. *Lead Yourself First: Inspiring Leadership Through Solitude.* (Bloomsbury, 2017). Pg. 182.
151 Collins, Jim and Morten T. Hansen. *Great by Choice: Uncertainty, Chaos, and Luck - Why Some Thrive Despite Them All.* (Harper Business, 2011).

mistaken or confused with another term, 'hazard.' When you decide to take a risk, it's not the risk that threatens you. Instead, it's the hazard. It's not the fall, but the sudden stop at the end. Risk is just an expression of probability that a hazard might occur. If you take a small risk, what you are really saying is that something hazardous could happen, but that it is not likely. If you take a big risk, you are really saying that there's a good chance that something awful will happen. What's implied in big risk taking is that the odds are against you and that you are likely to lose a lot if not everything. So, the question is, when do you take big risks? If you ask the best-selling business leadership guru of the past few decades, Jim Collins, he will tell you that it's probably never.

Renowned for writing one of the best-selling and deeply researched business books of all time, *Good to Great* (Harper Collins, 2005), Collins followed up with a 'sequel,' *Great by Choice* (Harper Business, 2011) that investigated the role of risk-taking in successful businesses. Studying what Collins and his co-author Morten T. Hansen labeled '10X' companies for those that had outperformed their industry by a factor of ten, they found something interesting. They discovered that 10X companies were risk averse. "They were not more risk taking, more bold, more visionary, and more creative than the comparisons," write the authors, "they were more *disciplined* [italics mine], more empirical, and more paranoid."[152] They found that 10X companies were smart about the risks they did take and fully understood the hazards involved. They acted in a manner that either negated, mitigated or altogether avoided identified hazards. They especially avoided what Collins and Hansen called "death line risks". They avoided risks that could have ruined the company.

Evaluating the hazards of any given decision or course of action, and estimating the risk involved is an essential skill for leaders. Risk appears romantic in hindsight only for those that got lucky. But, the preponderance of evidence demonstrates that good leaders make

---
152 Ibid. Pg. 9.

disciplined choices to control or avoid hazards. Guideline *K1 - Take action* should be taken within the context of judicious risk assessment. Threat or hazard analysis is an essential component of a good planning and decision-making process. It is the second of the six-step planning model within *Flawless Execution*. Only when the hazards have been identified and actively addressed as part of the plan, should a bias for action predominate.

Risk assessment gets pushed aside sometimes because it may be viewed from the lens of analysis paralysis. Although it certainly can deter action, leaders should view that analysis is an action itself, but with a suspense date (*K1*). Analysis is an important activity for leaders and their teams. As team performance and psychological safety expert Amy Edmondson cites, "Diagnosis, for example, is a form of action. And action at its best is a form of diagnosis." However, she continues, "One of the biggest mistakes managers make is conducting extensive diagnostic phases, ostensibly before acting, which can serve both to postpone the kind of critical learning that occurs from trying things out, and to obscure the fact that the diagnosis is itself an intervention."[153] That is the fine line between analysis and action that leaders must walk. It gets a lot easier to walk that line when the hazards and their probabilities are identified up front. Depending on their severity, leaders can determine how much analysis is warranted before acting.

ACTIONS:

Perform a risk assessment. Risk assessment isn't rocket science. You can conduct a simple risk assessment on the back of a cocktail napkin. A risk assessment model only needs a three-by-three grid with an x-axis labeled 'probability' and subdivided from left-to-right into three categories ranging from 'probable,' to 'may,' and finally to 'improbable.'

---

153 Edmondson, Amy. *Teaming: How Organizations Learn, Innovate, and Compete in the Knowledge Economy*. (Jossey-Bass, 2012). Pg. 242.

Then, label the y-axis in descending order from 'serious,' to 'minor,' and finally to 'negligible'. The definitions of each category are left ambiguous because assigning exact probabilities and hazards are contextually dependent from one team or organization to another. You can provide definitive parameters for each based upon your own needs. The idea is simply this—that you should not engage in probable risks that could invoke serious hazards that may even "kill the company." However, improbable things that could only cause negligible damage should usually be dismissed. It's the things that fall in between these two extremes that wise organizations act to mitigate, negate or avoid as part of their course of action. Making an intentional decision to go ahead ("go") or to terminate ("no go") a course of action is what this simple risk assessment model provides.

PROBABILITY

SEVERITY		PROBABLE	MAY	IMPROBABLE
	SERIOUS	NO GO	NO GO	CAUTION
	MINOR	NO GO	CAUTION	GO
	NEGLIGIBLE	CAUTION	GO	GO

Don't bet the company. In the introduction of this guideline, Collins and Hansen underscore in no uncertain terms the severe penalty paid by a failure to identify risks. They remind us that, "the only mistakes you can learn from are the ones you survive." Learning through the execution of plans is a fundamental assumption of much of this book. But, acting without a clear understanding of what's at stake or failing to take some action to mitigate the dangers, and learning won't matter. It may all be over after that. The lesson is to avoid, as Collins and Hansen put it, 'death line risk.' Or, in other words, don't bet the company!

CONCLUSION

Where to Point Your Finger First

I spent a weekend meeting, inspecting, and touring a military unit I would soon be taking over. Towards the end of that weekend, I followed my soon-to-be predecessor into the corner office she occupied, one I was looking forward to occupying soon myself. So far, I'd been pleased with everything I saw and everyone I'd met. We closed the door, preparing for a private meeting between in-coming and out-going leaders. I sat down across the desk from my host, a notebook open in my lap to a fresh, blank page. This was going to be a discussion about the senior leadership team and the members of the organization. She related to me her candid opinions and experiences about most everyone from the senior most-leaders, staff, the middle-management, on down to the front line. She had not a single positive thing to say about any one of them. All she offered was criticism and blame. At first, I took notes, but stopped after just a few minutes.

I knew there was something going on when I was selected for the new position. A senior leader and mentor had hinted but was wise enough to allow me the opportunity to see and identify it for myself. I knew there was a problem and I had heard it through the grapevine. Now I saw it clearly as it sat across the desk from me.

Whatever you may think of Napoleon Bonaparte, he certainly set the bar for leadership high. In guideline *L1*, I introduced a quote from the former French Emperor that bears repeating. He is attributed to have said that "There are no bad soldiers, only bad officers." It is daunting to accept responsibility for failures on your team. However, leaders benefit from extending their scope of responsibility beyond themselves and onto everyone they lead because otherwise they cannot identify shortcomings, resolve weaknesses, and address root causes. Leading is hard. It's not just hard work, it's tough on the emotions. It can be very rewarding, but also psychologically painful to good leaders that care about their team and their mission. If you are in a leadership position and think it's easy, then you are probably doing it wrong. If you find yourself blaming your team, then you should turn the finger of blame around and point it at yourself, first. A leader's default position should be to assume that they are the one that has erred. The best leaders find a way to improve. This book is intended to help them.

What About Inspiration?

With the full list of guidelines concluded, the reader might identify something missing, something obvious—inspiration. There's no guideline in this book that tells you to become a better leader by becoming a more inspirational leader. How does one become inspiring? Sure, it's a great quality to have as a leader, but how do you do it?

The introduction laid out this book's intent in terms of the quantifiable, prescriptive acts of leadership—the science rather than the art. Art defies easy description. Mastery of an art first requires mastery of its tools and techniques. Thus, this book has provided the essential tools and techniques of good leaders. For example, being an inspiring leader requires many of the guidelines presented herein. Inspiring leaders must be responsible models of behavior (*L1 & L3*). They should establish a vision, course of action and connect daily activities to that vision (*O4 & C2*). Inspiring leaders act with focus to a defined set of priorities (*K1, D1, & D2*). Doing all these things may fall short of inspiration in its highest form, but without them inspiration ultimately devolves into disillusionment. Inspiration is like a quick hit of caffeine. It may get people up and moving, but without the sustaining nourishment provided by the guidelines in this book, teams will hunger for something more substantial; the willful dedication to the soft technology of leadership day after day.

A Leadership Map?

This book attempts to provide an organized, comprehensive set of guidelines to leading high-performing teams. The reader might use it like a checklist and take an inventory of the actions and activities that they and their team do not do well. Leaders can then isolate single or groups of guidelines to implement more fully and improve performance. Overlapping and connected ideas have been indicated throughout. Thus, readers can isolate a single guideline and implement it in their daily leadership role or explore several related guidelines for a more comprehensive approach.

To aid the process of identifying the critical activities a team might employ to improve, a relationship map is provided on the following page. This *leadership map* is coded to correspond to the twenty-eight guidelines. It indicates direct relationships between guidelines with a solid line and supporting relationships with a dotted line. The first guideline, take responsibility (*L1*), is essential to every guideline and, therefore, is indicated as a central 'node' within the map with arrows emanating in all directions. There are other primary nodes that connect directly to many other guidelines. Those guidelines are: cultivate SA (*L4*), delegate and trust (*L6*); establish a course of action (*O4*), connect to the big picture (*C2*), take action (*K4*), and prioritize (*D1*). These guidelines provide great starting points for leaders who want to find the areas where they can make the most impactful changes to their leadership activities and the performance of their teams. Of course, the leadership map appears complicated. Actually, leadership is extremely complex. Remember that if you think it is easy, you are probably doing it wrong. The leadership map can help you navigate the challenge of leading well.

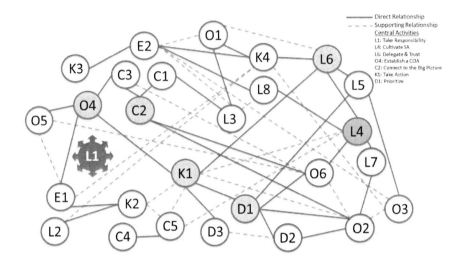

Leading Forward

Leadership is coaxing a pattern out of chaos, a pattern that the leader designs.[154] The pattern is a clear vision that is essential so that others, the led, can become leaders themselves and take up the responsibility of craftsmen that share that vision, help to evolve it, and work to bring it to fruition. It is a delicate art, especially in this VUCA world.

The pattern is the thing. As individuals, we imagine a pattern we desire for our own lives. We dream a picture of our future. However, that dream changes—sometimes quite radically—as we live our lives and grow older. What we want at ten, and twenty, and forty, and seventy years is different from what preceded. We change. What we value changes. Our roles change. We are not constant. Nothing is.

---

154 The use of the word "Chaos" is intentional. I use it for its scientific meaning rather than to suggest it is a synonym for disorder. Chaos is the natural state of the universe, a process that gives rise to ever-changing and newly emerging patterns.

The organizations we individual humans form are no different. They evolve and adapt over time. These organizations should have some clear reason, a mission, that provides some constancy over time, but the vision must evolve. It must change. Therefore, the activity of the organization must change, sometimes rapidly to keep pace with change in the environment.

Inevitably, a tension arises between the imagined pattern, the vision, and the pattern that emerges in the outside world. An organization's purpose is to shape these patterns into coherence. Both are changed by the effort, and new patterns—both imagined and real—emerge. To suggest that leading through this chaotic, unpredictable cause-and-effect maelstrom understates the challenge. Leadership is complex. As a prominent scientist, Scott Page, has put it, "Complexity is like trying to tame a lion while poking a tiger with a stick." Humans are complex organisms and, when grouped together into teams and organizations, the level of complexity only rises. Leading such complex networks of individuals may be the pinnacle of complex challenges.

Although leadership is truly a complex challenge, complex leadership methodologies only serve to increase the challenge. Instead, simplicity is the best approach. Simplicity beats complexity. Thus, this book has endeavored to reduce the complexity of leadership to a set of simple guidelines. When paired with the *Flawless Execution* methodology, briefly described in *Appendix A*, leaders possess a powerfully effective technology, a system, to aid in the work of leadership. As the pace of technological innovation quickens, the much more stable patterns of human behavior and interaction have become ever more important. Leaders that can harness an understanding of these behavioral patterns, employ proven guidelines and processes built upon generations of experience and proven by continuously emerging cognitive science, stand a good chance of crafting and achieving their visions.

These guidelines and methodologies, as with anything, do evolve and change. But, because their object—the human being—evolves imperceptibly slow compared to the lightning-quick change in the technology, these guidelines serve as a bedrock technology that changes at a geologically slow pace. It is unfortunate then, that the human dimension of technology is often called 'soft' as opposed to the 'hard' technology we can physically touch and hold in our hand. As addressed in the sections on knowledge and experience, this is a book that seeks to transform *know-how* into *know-what*. Leaders benefit deeply from experience, but that doesn't mean that inexperienced leaders cannot benefit as deeply from the supporting soft technology provided herein.

Only a decade or so ago, a buzz phrase was *change management*. This phrase appears to ignore two important aspects of change. The first is that change is continuous rather than transitory. The ancient Greek philosopher, Heraclitus, remarked that "change is the only constant in life." The other is that change can or should be managed as if it were like managing an infestation of cockroaches in an office building.

Change is continuous. It is a fundamental law of the universe that all good leaders must confront. If they ignore it, they are doomed. If they merely manage or respond to it, they will remain at least one step behind it. However, for leaders that harness the forces of change, develop a clear vision of the future, and undertake intentional efforts to shape it, success is possible. Good leaders not only recognize the inevitability of change, but also welcome the opportunities it brings.

If you believe you can exercise leadership as a masterful art form without a system or process to help, you are probably taking on more than you can handle. Leaders need systems to help them and their teams. John Wooden built a leadership system to help his UCLA basketball team become champions year-over-year. Every organization needs a system to create value for its clients and customers. Without systems you are doomed to recreating success from the ground up every day. That is too daunting and inefficient to be effective. Leaders must create the system necessary for success. It is usually a slow process too often informed by mistakes and failures. However, smart leaders can learn from others and from science. Those leaders can take the accumulated wisdom presented herein to develop their own system, one that works best for them in their unique context and according to their unique personality. This book offers a foundational system for leaders to take and adapt as they deem fit.

Leadership is most characterized by vision and people. Those are its most essential aspects. Without some defined goal and a group of people to achieve it, there is no leadership. Because these two aspects imply immense complexity, leadership cannot be reduced to a set of algorithms. Guideline 01 - *Develop and execute standards* addresses the spectrum between the certitude of the algorithm and the ambiguity of the guideline or heuristic. It is this author's hope that this book provides at least the necessary guidelines and some useful instructions on exercising leadership. The guidelines are few and simple while the instructions, provided as *actions* in each section, are a small portion of a potentially infinite list of techniques to improve leadership.

Although patterns recur, nothing is ever exactly the same in the complex world of human interaction. Readers of this book cannot simply apply a *wax on and wax off* approach to the art of leadership as Daniel did in the *Karate Kid*. Readers should take this book as a guide only. They should apply its guidelines consistently, but always through the lens of good judgment.

As I write these final lines, I am reminded of a witty bit of wisdom I saw on a t-shirt recently. The inscription, transformed a bit from an original quote by Mark Twain, read: "Good judgment comes from wisdom and wisdom…comes from bad judgment." A book can only serve as a guide. You must act in the real world to gain the experience that, ultimately, informs good judgment. And that experience can be painful. I hope this book helps the reader avoid some of that pain for their own sake and for the sake of those they lead.

APPENDIX A – THE FLAWLESS EXECUTION METHODOLOGY

What is Flawless Execution?

Flawless Execution is defined as *a holistic framework of simple, interdependent processes that enable individuals, teams and organizations to accelerate performance in the rapidly changing, challenging, and complex world.*

Following centuries of development in warfare, over 60 years of groundbreaking work in neuroscience and cognitive psychology, and two decades of further development and application, Flawless Execution is a cutting-edge methodology for individuals, teams, and organizations to excel in the volatile, uncertain, complex, and ambiguous (VUCA) modern world.

Flawless Execution is *simple*. It must be simple if everyone in the organization is going to use it. But it also must be simple because, in a complex world, complicated and complex solutions only make challenges more difficult. In the modern world, *simplicity beats complexity*.

Flawless Execution is also *scalable*. An individual can use it to improve personally and professionally; a team can use it to create high performance; and it scales to the entire organization to empower long-term success and continuous improvement.

In this brief overview, you will learn about the Flawless Execution *Model* and The Flawless Execution *Cycle*. What's the difference? The Flawless Execution Model is a simple pyramid-shaped model. It's the model for applying Flawless Execution at its grandest scale across an enterprise. In the center of that pyramid is the Flawless Execution cycle, or 'engine,' which is the iterative cycle of *plan, brief, execute* and *debrief* that empowers the rest of the model.

The engine that lies at the heart of Flawless Execution is easy to learn and employ so teams can remain agile in a continually changing environment. It accepts that errors and failures are inevitable in a complex environment. It uses both failures and successes to learn, improve and adapt continuously.

Furthermore, iterating in short cycles so that one can adapt quickly is essential. Modern teams must be able to develop lessons learned and spread them throughout the organization to stay ahead of the rate of change.

To do that, a methodology must be simple. The Flawless Execution Cycle is just four processes—plan, brief, execute, and debrief—each made up of 5 to 7 smaller steps. It is easy to learn and apply by everyone from the most senior executives to the front-line teams of the organization and laterally throughout its many functions and divisions. Everyone can use it and benefit from it.

Because it's easy to learn and fundamental to succeeding in complex environments, it is scalable. The front-line customer service agent and the young new hire can use it just as well as the C-suite executive. It is the same basic process for an individual planning their day to the CEO planning the next three years.

Unlike the multitude of other methodologies such as Lean Six Sigma, Scrum, the project management body of knowledge or PMBOK, and many, many more, Flawless Execution is a universally applicable methodology that can be used with or in support of other specialized and more complicated methodologies.

Since its development, the Flawless Execution model has been utilized in every industry and endeavor including: business operations, manufacturing, retail, banking, heavy industry, oil & gas, mining, construction, healthcare, information technology, sales organizations, project management, professional athletics, and youth programs.

Overview of the Flawless Execution Cycle

At the core of the Flawless Execution Model is the engine that powers it, the Flawless Execution Cycle. The cycle is: plan, brief, execute, and debrief.

Each of these four main components contains a set of 5 to 7 steps or techniques. What follows is an overview of those basic processes.

Plan. There are six steps to the planning methodology. Supporting this method is a process of structured collaboration called *Teamstorming*[SM] to help teams engage and build a good plan quickly.

- First, determine your mission objective—what specifically is it that you are trying to accomplish?
- Second, identity the threats, obstacles or challenges that stand in the way of accomplishing your objective.

- Third, shift your thinking and identify the resources you have available to you or may need to acquire to accomplish the objective.
- Fourth, evaluate lessons learned that are relevant to your objective. These lessons learned are the output of regular debriefing.
- Fifth, determine a course of action – the actual tasks that must be accomplished to achieve your objective.
- Sixth, and finally, plan for contingencies. Contingencies are pre-planned responses to things that may go wrong.

Brief. Briefing is an important part of the Flawless Execution Cycle. It is one of the four primary stand-alone activities. It is also used in support of the plan and execute phases as well. The briefing process follows a simple and easy to remember acronym, B.R.I.E.F, which stands for:

> B – Big Picture; brief the scenario
>
> R – Review the mission objective
>
> I – Identify the threats and resources
>
> E – Execution, the course of action
>
> F – Flexibilities or contingencies

Execute. There are many tools and techniques within the 'Execute' phase of the cycle. One of the primary challenges to overcome during execution is task saturation[SM]: the perception or reality that you have too much to do and too little time, talent or resources to accomplish it all. Many of the tools are designed to help negate, mitigate or manage task saturation. Some of these are: checklists, cross-checks, mutual support, task shedding, *execution rhythm*[SM], and *X-Gap Meetings*[SM].

Debrief. Debriefing is one of the most powerful processes in Flawless Execution. New research has proven its incredible value. Debriefing follows a seven-step process called 'Stealth.' S.T.E.A.L.T.H is an acronym that helps you remember the proper steps. Those steps are:

    S – Set the Time

    T – Tone

    E – Execution vs. Objectives

    A – Analyze Execution

    L – Lesson Learned

    T – Transfer Lessons Learned

    H - High Note

Overview of the Flawless Execution Model

The Flawless Execution Cycle is a simple model—and so is the Flawless Execution Model. The model has three tiers: the *platform*, the *process*, and the *purpose*. You have already been introduced to the *process*—the Flawless Execution Cycle. The Cycle, or engine, nurtures and enables the other two tiers to learn and adapt in an agile manner.

At the bottom is the *platform*. People are the foundation and the most important part of the model. Not only do you have to get the right people on the bus, as management and leadership scholar Jim Collins has written, you also must empower them, engage them, and enable them to learn continuously. That is what the model and cycle do for the people of the organization.

Of course, people must be trained. Training is a subset of learning. Knowing how and what to train them on is an ever-changing and evolving process that is also identified through the Flawless Execution Cycle.

Then, as any high-performing organization knows, standards or standard operating procedures are essential to scale and sustain success. Standards are always evolving and adapting to changing demands.

At the top of the Flawless Execution model is the *purpose* tier. At the very top of that there is the vision of the organization—but not in the same format as many organizations will describe it. In Flawless Execution, describing an organization's vision of the future requires designing that future with detail. Thus, in Flawless Execution, vision is called a *high-definition destination* or HDD. An HDD is a holistic description of the future in certain key areas. The HDD is essential to align the organization—to remind everyone what they are ultimately working toward.

Then there is strategy. Strategy, which is described in terms of *critical leverage points* or CLP's, tells the organization how it will achieve its HDD.

Finally, there is *leader's intent*. In both the HDD and in strategic plans, objectives are described first as intent, a subjective formulation of what is intended to be accomplished. Then, objective measurements are developed that provide indicators of success of the intended effect. This allows teams and individuals to act with greater autonomy, utilizing their own expertise and good judgment to achieve results. As behavioral and cognitive scientists now know, autonomy is essential to getting creativity and engagement from knowledge workers.

For more detail and direction on implementing the Flawless Execution methodology, refer to The Flawless Execution Field Manual, 2nd Edition by James D. Murphy and William M. Duke or at www.afterburner.com.

APPENDIX B: SUMMARY OF GUIDELINES

LEADERSHIP

L1 - Take responsibility
- Reflect
- Lead upward

L2 - Get the right people on your team
- Pick a leader
- Align attitude and values
- Seek diversity
- Stay lean
- Build the team

L3 - Model appropriate behaviors
- Put on your uniform
- Call out behaviors
- Commit publicly

L4 - Cultivate situational awareness
- Share intentionally
- Hold a standup
- Train SA
- Debrief at all levels
- Pick People's Brains

L5 - Facilitate collaboration
- Leaders speak last
- Individuals think first

- Think ahead
- Think early
- Optimize size
- Take Time for Pie

L6 - Delegate and trust
- Plan to small wins

L7 - Orchestrate mutual support
- Walk around
- Talk Across the seams
- Attitude pledge

L8 - Thank and reward
- Recognize the deed
- Do it publicly
- Do it infrequently
- Do it now
- Do it justly
- Peers do it best

ORGANIZATION

O1 - Develop and execute standards
- Few and simple
- Visible and accessible
- Execute to standards
- Validate and maintain

O2 - Align roles to goals
- Define purpose, vision, and strategy
- Set goals

- Define roles
- Post progress publicly

O3 - Measurements follow intent
- Describe intent, first
- Determine measurements, second

O4 - Establish a course of action
- Utilize a rational process

O5 - Plan for contingencies
- What could go wrong?
- How will you know when it does?
- What will you do?

O6 - Establish interactive *execution rhythm*[SM]
- Identify peak times
- Establish rhythm
- Close execution gaps

COMMUNICATION

C1 - Establish / reinforce organizational Identity
- Define purpose
- Articulate values
- Check performance

C2 - Connect to the big picture
- Connect purpose, vision, strategy, and tactics
- Envision success

C3 - Brief every plan
- Communicate the vision

- Use consistent structure

C4 - Establish a communication plan
- Define the lexicon
- Determine channels, use, and priorities
- Identify critical communications
- Organize for brevity
- Engineer chit-chat

C5 - Listen actively
- Listen to one person daily
- Focus on the speaker
- Vent in private

KNOWLEDGE

K1 - Take action
- Bias to act
- Set suspense

K2 - Include Expertise and diversity
- Diversity of experience
- Diversity of background
- Diversity of personality
- Get front-line input

K3 - Learn every day
- Watch, listen, read
- Coach and be coached
- Share learning

K4 - Train and develop

- Close training gaps
- Stop leading ... sometimes

EXPERIENCE

E1 - Red team
- *Quid pro quo*
- Conduct a formal red team

E2 – Assess to iterate, improve and accelerate experience
- Leaders admit errors
- Debrief to identify and learn from root causes

DISCIPLINE

D1 – Prioritize
- Design the future
- Identify a strategy
- Importance and Urgency
- Task Shed

D2 – Focus
- Schedule wisely
- Set expectations of availability

D3 - Risk Smart
- Perform a risk assessment
- Don't bet the company